DRACULA

Bram Stoker

adapted by David Calcutt

OXFORD
UNIVERSITY PRESS

OXFORD
UNIVERSITY PRESS

Great Clarendon Street, Oxford OX2 6DP

Oxford University Press is a department of the University of Oxford.
It furthers the University's objective of excellence in research,
scholarship, and education by publishing worldwide in

Oxford New York

Auckland Bangkok Buenos Aires Cape Town Chennai
Dar es Salaam Delhi Hong Kong Istanbul Karachi Kolkata
Kuala Lumpur Madrid Melbourne Mexico City Mumbai Nairobi
São Paulo Shanghai Taipei Tokyo Toronto

Oxford is a registered trade mark of Oxford University Press
in the UK and in certain other countries

British Library Cataloguing in Publication Data

Data available

30 29 28 27 26 25 24 23 22

ISBN 978 019 831898 9

Typeset by Fakenham Photosetting, Fakenham, Norfolk

Printed and bound by Bell and Bain Ltd, Glasgow

Acknowledgements

The Publisher would like to thank the following for permission to
reproduce photographs:
Ronald Grant Archive: page 124 (left); Kobal Collection: page 124
(middle); Moviestore: page 124 (right).

The artwork is by Peter Melnyczuk.

Cover image © AF archive/Alamy

MIX
Paper from
responsible sources
FSC® C007785
www.fsc.org

Contents

General Introduction

With a fresh, modern look, this classroom-friendly series boasts an exciting range of authors – from Pratchett to Chaucer – whose works have been expertly adapted by such well-known and popular writers as Philip Pullman and David Calcutt.

Many teachers use Oxford *Playscripts* to study the format, style, and structure of playscripts with their students; for speaking and listening assignments; to initiate discussion of relevant issues in class; to cover Drama as part of the curriculum; as an introduction to the novel of the same title; and to introduce the less able or willing to pre-1914 literature.

At the back of each Oxford *Playscript*, you will find a brand new Activity section, which not only addresses the points above, but also features close text analysis, and activities that provide support for underachieving readers and act as a springboard for personal writing.

Many schools will simply read through the play in class with no staging at all, and the Activity sections have been written with this in mind, with individual activities ranging from debates and designing campaign posters to writing extra scenes or converting parts of the original novels into playscript form.

For those of you, however, who do wish to take to the stage, we have included, where necessary, 'A Note on Staging' – a section dedicated to suggesting ways of staging the play, as well as examining the props and sets you may wish to use.

Above all, we hope you will enjoy using Oxford *Playscripts*, be it on the stage or in the classroom.

WHAT THE ADAPTER SAYS

One of the first challenges I faced when I started out was how to make this adaptation of *Dracula* different from every version that had come before. It's not that I believe in changing things, or making things different simply for the sake of it. But there have been so many versions of Bram Stoker's novel, for the stage, the radio and – most widely and popularly – for the screen, that the Count himself has become almost a cliché. Also, quite apart from *Dracula*, recently there has been a revival of interest in vampire stories generally – mainly in film and television – and each of these versions has explored the legend in its own way. When I started out, I really did wonder whether there was anything new to say about the subject.

The job of an adapter isn't simply to re-tell the original story in play form. The adapter must engage with the story, find something in it that connects with his or her own interests – even obsessions. However faithfully you follow the original, it's inevitable that your version will be coloured by your own particular vision of that story and its themes. The Dracula of Bram Stoker's novel isn't the suave charmer who appears in later films. He's a beast, a monster without a soul. I felt the Dracula who appears in the novel was two-dimensional – he's not a fully-developed character. I wanted to know why Dracula was doing what he was doing. I wanted to tell some of the story from his viewpoint. Bram Stoker's novel is very much a product of its time: for the Victorians, Dracula was a thing of pure evil, to be destroyed at all cost. But we've come to see what we call 'evil' in a different light. We condemn it, but we also try to understand what causes it – what makes a person evil.

The Dracula in the play is much less clear-cut, much more ambiguous, than the Dracula in the novel. His actions are horrific, but at the same time we can feel sorry for him. And he also holds out to Mina the promise of eternal life, complete freedom. At the end of the play, she's had a glimpse of something she can never forget. She's started to understand Dracula.

The novel of *Dracula* is packed and crowded with incident, character, and detail, far too much and far too complex to include in a play. A play by its nature needs to be clear, simple, and precise – otherwise it loses its focus, its drama. So, the next problem was what to cut, what to leave out, and how to shape the story around a few intense dramatic moments. For a long time I didn't know and made several false starts. Whenever that happens, I decide that the only way out of the corner I've got myself into is to take drastic action. I decided to pull the whole novel inside-out, so to speak, and start the play halfway through the original story, with Mina and Lucy in England. This had the desired effect. It helped make the play in part my own creation, and I was able to start writing seriously.

In fact, in the end, I actually went back more or less to the original structure of the novel – starting with Jonathan's journey to Castle Dracula – but that initial kick-start had the effect of placing the two women, and especially Mina, at the centre of the action. And this made me realize that, in my version at least, the central dramatic conflict would be between Mina and Dracula, and that it would be Mina, not the men, who would finally bring about Dracula's defeat and destruction. I was very excited by this idea, and felt that, at last, I'd found a fresh way of looking at the story, a way to revitalize it, and re-make it as if new. Then I discovered that one of the first film versions of the novel – a silent film of the 1920s called *Nosferatu* – had done just this very thing! So, perhaps there are no new ways of looking at things after all. Only old ways.

David Calcutt

ABOUT THE AUTHOR

Bram Stoker was born in November 1847 in Dublin. As a child, he was ill and spent long hours in bed. During this time, his mother Charlotte told him Irish fairy stories and true accounts of the horrors of the cholera epidemic she had witnessed during her own childhood. No one really knows what was wrong with Bram, but he made a complete recovery and grew to be a fit and energetic young man.

In 1864, Stoker went to Trinity college, Dublin, where he became a popular student and a good athlete. He also developed a passion for the theatre. In 1867, he saw the famous actor Henry Irving performing at the Theatre Royal, Dublin. This experience had a huge and lasting effect on Bram Stoker.

After gaining his degree, he became a civil servant. But in 1871 he saw Irving again at the Vaudeville Theatre. He was so impressed with Irving's performance that he decided to become a theatre critic and offered his services free of charge to the *Dubin Mail.*

About this time he began to take an interest in vampires. He read vampire stories by other authors and started to think about writing his own vampire tale. In 1875, he published his first 'horror' story – *The Chain of Destiny.*

In 1876, Henry Irving returned to Dublin to play Hamlet. Stoker wrote glowing reviews of Irving's performance, which led to a meeting between the two. Irving asked Stoker to become his business manager in London. Before leaving Dublin, Stoker resigned from the civil service and married Florence Balcombe, a neighbour who had also been courted by the writer Oscar Wilde.

Stoker worked long hours for Irving, but he still made time to continue his research on vampires and other 'gothic' themes. He continued to write horror stories for adults and children. In 1890, he started work on *Dracula.* During the next few years he spent summer holidays at Whitby in North Yorkshire and at Cruden Bay in Scotland. Both places were to

ABOUT THE AUTHOR

DRACULA

7

influence descriptions and events in the novel he was writing. Dracula was published in 1897.

In 1905, Henry Irving collapsed and died. This had a dramatic effect on Stoker, who suffered a stroke. His employer's death signalled the end of his contract and so Stoker had to write more fiction to earn a living. He finished his final novel, *The Lair of the White Worm*, in 1911. He died a year later from 'exhaustion', aged 64.

A Note on Staging

Adapter's Introduction

Before you read the play, you might find it useful to know what I had in mind when I wrote the script. The story of *Dracula* unfolds in two ways:

- through a number of narrators who describe the events as they experienced them
- by showing the actual events as they happen.

I have kept the set design, the props, the lighting instructions, and the stage directions to a minimum in the script – and the play can be read aloud in the classroom or performed for an audience successfully using these directions alone. But there are occasions, particularly during the narrated sections of the playscript, when you may decide that additional movement, mime, or props are appropriate.

Equally, you may choose to use more scenery, furniture, props, special effects (such as dry ice), or sound than I have suggested; or you may have a sophisticated lighting system at your disposal (the existing lighting directions are there simply as a guide). The decision as to how you produce your performance of *Dracula* is up to you, and the structure of this playscript allows for this.

Costumes and Props

Props you may need include:

Mr Hawkins:	a file of papers.
Jonathan:	a briefcase; money.
Landlady:	a small crucifix on a chain.
Lost girl:	a hood.
Count Dracula:	a photograph of Mina
Hags:	hoods.
Renfield:	a small box.
Lucy:	a shawl; a brooch.
Van Helsing:	a crucifix.
Seward:	a small carpet bag.
Mina:	a lace shawl; a small crucifix on a chain.

The Play at a Glance

The outline of the play below highlights the props or scenery you may want to consider for a performance.

Throughout

There should be a large French window with double doors at the centre rear of the stage. This can be hidden by a large deep red curtain, and revealed when it is needed – as in the scenes where Dracula enters and exits through the window to appear to both Lucy and Mina. Other characters (including Dracula, where appropriate) enter and exit from the sides of the stage, which should be hung with large red drapes. A bench or seat should be placed just off to one side of the window, to the stage left.

CHARACTERS

Count Dracula	a Transylvanian aristocrat; also a vampire
Jonathan Harker	a young lawyer; engaged to **Mina**
Mr Hawkins	a solicitor; **Jonathan's** employer
Landlady	at the Golden Krone Hotel in Bistritz, Transylvania
a lost girl	whom **Jonathan** meets on his way to Castle Dracula
Mina Murray	an intelligent young woman; engaged to **Jonathan**
Lucy Westenra	**Mina's** friend since childhood; lives in Whitby
Dr John Seward	a young doctor in charge of a large asylum in Whitby; one of **Lucy's** admirers
Quincey Morris	a well-travelled young American; a friend of **John Seward** and **Arthur Holmwood**; also admires **Lucy**
Arthur Holmwood	only son of Lord Godalming; engaged to **Lucy**
Hag 1 **Hag 2** **Hag 3**	hideous creatures at Castle Dracula
Mr Swales	Whitby's oldest inhabitant
Reporter	on Whitby's newspaper
Coastguard	at Whitby
Renfield	a patient at **Doctor Seward's** asylum
Bennett **Withers**	attendants who work at the asylum
Mrs Westenra	**Lucy's** mother
Professor Van Helsing	once **Doctor Seward's** tutor; an expert on vampires
a child	a boy who plays in the abbey churchyard as it gets dark
Mrs Outhwaite	caretaker at Carfax Manor

PROLOGUE

The lights rise. **Dracula** *enters and speaks to the audience.*

Dracula

For centuries I have walked my world alone. In fierce joy, but in weariness too. The weariness of solitude. For so long I have yearned for a companion to share with me this world, this eternity. And I shall walk alone no more. One shall walk beside me. One shall become my companion. Here, beneath this sky lit by its numberless stars, we shall stand together, and gaze towards the black shadows of the mountains. And we shall be filled with hunger and silent longing, and the moon shall rise, and we shall be wolves running, with the horizons rolling endlessly beneath our feet.

Dracula goes.

A CT 1

● ●

SCENE 1

Jonathan Harker enters carrying a briefcase. He puts this down and speaks to the audience.

Jonathan   It began when I was working as an assistant lawyer in the offices of Mr Hawkins, the solicitor. And it was in connection with that work, and from Mr Hawkins's own lips, that I first heard the name of Dracula.

Mr Hawkins enters, carrying a file of papers. He speaks to Jonathan.

Mr Hawkins   He lives in Eastern Europe. A small country called Transylvania. Ever heard of it?

Jonathan turns to Mr Hawkins.

Jonathan   No, I can't say that I have.

Mr Hawkins   Neither had I. It doesn't matter. Bohemia, Moravia, Muldavia, Transylvania – all places on a map between here and there, if you know what I mean.

Jonathan   Yes . . .

Mr Hawkins   Anyway, this Dracula fellow lives there. An aristocrat. Old family, going all the way back to the time of Attila the Hun, or something like that. And the point is, he wants to move to England. Fallen in love with the place, by all accounts. All from books, mind. Never been here. No doubt he'll find the reality a bit different.

Jonathan   No doubt.

Mr Hawkins   None of his craggy mountains and pine forests and wild landscapes here. Corner shops and trolley-buses. And rain. We mustn't forget the rain. Not that we could if we tried.

Pause.

Where was I?

Jonathan	You were telling me about Mr Dracula.
Mr Hawkins	Count ... Count Dracula, my boy. No plain 'Mr' for him. Oh, dear me, no. These European chaps can be very touchy about their ancestry and titles. Remember that when you meet him.
Jonathan	I'm to meet him?
Mr Hawkins	Yes. That's what I'm coming to. You see, he got in touch with me a while back through an agent of his – can't remember the man's name. English, he was. Very excitable, though. Couldn't keep still. Made my head spin just to speak with him. Well, this agent brought me a letter from the Count stating that he wished to move to England and he wanted a reliable firm to find a place for him. Money no object. A reliable firm, my boy. And he chose us. How's that, eh?
Jonathan	Your reputation's travelled far indeed, Mr Hawkins.
Mr Hawkins	So it would appear. And so shall you, Jonathan. You shall travel with it. All the way to Transylvania!
Jonathan	What? I'm to go there?
Mr Hawkins	Yes! That's what I'm trying to tell you. I think I've found just the kind of place Count Dracula is looking for. Not an easy task, I can tell you. He was very particular in his requirements. Very particular. Quite odd, some of them, too. Still, it's not my place to comment on a client's wishes. Especially when that client is paying so handsomely.
Jonathan	Where is the place you've found?
Mr Hawkins	Oh. It's in the north. Whitby.
Jonathan	*[Surprised]* Really?
Mr Hawkins	Do you know it?
Jonathan	No, but my fiancée is going there this summer, to stay with an old friend of hers.
Mr Hawkins	Coincidence, eh? She'll come across this place. Carfax Manor,

it's called. A bit of a ruin, really, but that's what he asked for. Something old and spacious and remote. Well, Carfax Manor is certainly old and spacious, and you can't get much more remote than Whitby!

Jonathan   You've written and told the Count?

Mr Hawkins   I have, and he's written back, and asked me to travel to his home with all the details and documents. As if it were like hopping into a cab across town. I'm too old for such a journey, but you're not, so I'm sending you in my place. It's about time you saw something of the world.

Jonathan   I'm very grateful, Mr Hawkins. To be entrusted with such a responsibility – it's . . . a great honour.

Mr Hawkins   I wouldn't send you if I didn't think you were up to it, Jonathan. And you are. You're more than up to it. Why, sending you is like going myself. You have my every confidence. I've written a letter to the Count and told him so.

Jonathan   Thank you.

Mr Hawkins hands the file to Jonathan.

Hawkins   Everything's in there – details and specifications of the property, a photograph of it that I took myself, copies of the

deeds, documents – and contracts. Most importantly the contracts. There are three for him to sign. And there are travel arrangements sent by the Count. Study everything carefully. Put aside your other duties and devote yourself to this task. Have it all by heart by the time you arrive there. He'll expect as much, and so shall I.

Jonathan	When shall I leave?
Mr Hawkins	As soon as possible. Next week, if you can. The sooner you go, the sooner you'll be there, and the sooner back with everything signed and sealed. And then … well, I think you might have cause for celebration. And I'm not just talking about your forthcoming marriage. I'm looking for a partner, you know. Someone to run the business with me. Do well in this, and there'll be cause for celebration indeed.
Jonathan	*[Deeply grateful]* Thank you, Mr Hawkins.
Mr Hawkins	We'll talk further when you return. It's all in your hands, now.

Mr Hawkins turns to go. He stops and turns back.

Mr Hawkins	It's a great opportunity for you, my boy. A great opportunity. Yes. And a great adventure!

Mr Hawkins goes. Jonathan puts the file in his briefcase and as he does so he speaks to the audience.

Jonathan	A great adventure. So it seemed to me, too. Even the distress I felt at having to part from Mina, my fiancée, couldn't quell my sense of excitement and anticipation. And we told each other that it wouldn't be for long, and that, when I returned, we'd be married. So I left the next week, took the boat from Calais, went on to Paris, travelled by train to Munich, then onward to Budapest. From there, my journey was by coach, along roads increasingly remote, which wound their way through the Carpathian mountains. And at last, among the lower slopes of those mountains, I arrived at my penultimate destination, the town of Bistritz, and the Golden Krone Hotel, where I was to stay before setting out on the final stage of my journey.

*The **Landlady** enters and approaches **Jonathan**. She speaks with an Eastern European accent.*

Landlady	English?
Jonathan	Yes, that's right.
Landlady	It's a long way you've come. England is far from here.
Jonathan	It is. Very far.
Landlady	You speak good German.
Jonathan	Thank you.
Landlady	A good job. There's no one speaks English here. How long will you stay?
Jonathan	Just the one night. I have to go on, tomorrow, through the Borgo Pass. Is there a coach that will take me?
Landlady	Yes, there is a coach. It leaves here at four tomorrow afternoon, to Bukovina. Is that where you're going?
Jonathan	No. I only wish to go as far as the Borgo Pass.
Landlady	But there is nothing there.
Jonathan	I was told there's a road that leads to the Castle Dracula.

*The **Landlady** starts a little.*

Landlady	Castle Dracula?
Jonathan	Yes. That's where I'm going. You know it?
Landlady	I know it.
Jonathan	And there is a road – ?
Landlady	A track. It is not easy to walk.
Jonathan	Is it far, though? To the castle?
Landlady	*[Hesitantly]* No ...
Jonathan	Then I'm sure I'll manage –

Landlady	But the pass is many hours away. It will be dark when you get there.
Jonathan	I don't mind.
Landlady	If I'm permitted to ask, why do you go to Castle Dracula?
Jonathan	I have business with the Count.
Landlady	Business. Must you go there tomorrow?
Jonathan	Yes, I must.
Landlady	Stay here. One night is such a short time. Our town is beautiful. Stay a little longer, two nights. Go the day after tomorrow.
Jonathan	I wish I could. Your town does indeed look very beautiful. But my business is quite pressing. Perhaps when I come back –
Landlady	Do you know what tomorrow is?
Jonathan	It's the ... fourth of May –
Landlady	St George's Eve. On that day, and on that night, the evil things of the world have sway. They rise, they walk abroad, they are strong in their power. And that place to which you are going –

She stops.

Jonathan	What of it?
Landlady	It is old. Many dead lie in its roots. It has eaten much blood.
Jonathan	Look, I ... I'm afraid I don't believe in such things ...
Landlady	No, not in your land, perhaps. You have no need. But here there is need. It is not your land. It is ours, and here such things are real.

Jonathan turns and speaks to the audience.

Jonathan	Despite her obvious concern, I insisted I must travel on the next day. And seeing my determination, she fell silent, and showed me to my room. I passed a quiet night, and a pleasant

18

morning, and she spoke no more of her fears, until the carriage arrived and I prepared to take my leave.

*The **Landlady** speaks to **Jonathan**.*

Landlady	You are certain about going? You are decided?
Jonathan	Yes, I am.
Landlady	Then take this.

*She takes a small crucifix on a chain from her pocket and offers it to **Jonathan**.*

It is a cross, the sign of Our Lord and Saviour.

Jonathan	Really, I couldn't –
Landlady	Please. Take it. For your safety. It will protect you.

*She makes to fasten the cross around **Jonathan's** neck. He speaks sharply.*

Jonathan	No! I mean ... *[Changing his tone]* Yes, I will take it, thank you ... you're very kind ...

He takes the crucifix from her.

Landlady	Keep it with you at all times.
Jonathan	I will.
Landlady	And may God and His Holy Mother be with you, and keep you from evil.

*The **Landlady** turns and goes. **Jonathan** looks at the crucifix and speaks to the audience.*

Jonathan	I placed the crucifix in my pocket, and forgot about it. And I must have lost it, for I never saw it again.

He puts the crucifix in his pocket and picks up his briefcase. He then continues his story.

Within a short time of leaving the town, the sun began to set. As we climbed higher through the pass, the mountains were bathed in a deep red light, and the sky darkened above them, filling the whole world about me in shadow. Then I slept, and woke to darkness and black night. The carriage had stopped. We had reached the top of the Borgo Pass. I got out, found the road easily enough, and began my ascent to Castle Dracula. The landlady of the hotel had been right. It was hard going, especially at night. And cold, too. Bitterly cold. It was a cloudless night and the moon was full. In the distance I heard wolves howling. Once, I thought I saw a light flickering among the rocks above me. A pale-blue, unearthly light. I left the path and climbed towards it, but it disappeared, and as I turned to make my way back to the road, there was a movement in the shadows, and a figure stood before me.

*The **lost girl** enters and approaches **Jonathan**. She is dressed in rags and her face is hidden by a hood.*

Lost girl	Help me.

Jonathan turns to her, but continues to speak to the audience.

Jonathan	It was a girl – or young woman –
Lost girl	Will you help me?
Jonathan	Dressed in rags – her face hidden by a hood –
Lost girl	Please . . . help me.
Jonathan	And speaking so pitifully, her voice frail and weak –
Lost girl	I'm lost – I don't know where I am – what is this place?
Jonathan	She held her hand out towards me, imploring – a thin, white hand –
Lost girl	*[Holding out her hand to Jonathan]* You will help me? I'm so alone. So lost and alone. So cold, so hungry.

She moves closer to him.

Jonathan	A hand more bone than flesh – and nails so long – like claws –

*The **lost girl's** voice suddenly becomes a savage snarl.*

Lost girl	Lost and alone and cold and hungry!

20

*She lunges forward at **Jonathan**, her hands like claws, as if to tear at him. He cries out and falls back. At that moment, **Dracula** enters.*

Dracula No!

*The **lost girl** turns sharply, sees him, and hisses in fear. She cowers back from **Jonathan** as **Dracula** advances on her.*

Not him! Go! Be gone from here! Go, I say! Feed elsewhere tonight!

*Hissing and whimpering miserably, like an animal, the **lost girl** backs off and goes. **Dracula** turns and speaks to **Jonathan**.*

Mr Harker? You are Mr Jonathan Harker, from England?

Jonathan *[Still shaken and confused]* Yes …

Dracula I am Count Dracula. I thought you might be lost and came to meet you. It was fortunate I did, I think. Are you all right?

Jonathan Yes … just –

Dracula Of course. You should not have left the road, Mr Harker. It was a mistake. In these parts, one should never leave the road. It is not wise.

Jonathan That girl. Who is she?

Dracula A girl. An orphan. She has lived here in the mountains since her parents died. There was plague. Her mind is crazed. There is no real harm in her.

Jonathan She seemed frightened of you.

Dracula Yes.

There is a pause.

Come, now, Mr Harker. Let us go back to the road. My home is not far. We have had a poor meeting. I will try to make it up to you. Some food and wine, and a good night's sleep and you will feel, I am sure, fully recovered after your … shock.

Dracula turns from Jonathan, moves a little way off, and remains still as Jonathan speaks to the audience.

Jonathan	I followed him to the road, and then on to his home – a tall, imposing castle, built on top of a great crag. I didn't really take much of it in, then. I was tired, and still shaken after my ... experience. But I felt better after I'd eaten, and thanked the Count, and said to him that I assumed we'd begin going through the documents the next day.

Dracula turns and speaks to Jonathan.

Dracula	Unfortunately, no. I have to be away during the day on business. I will not be here when you wake. But I shall take the documents with me, and we can go through them together when I return.
Jonathan	When will that be?
Dracula	In the evening.
Jonathan	I see.
Dracula	For tomorrow, my home is yours. There will be food prepared. Spend the day as you wish. I'm sure you will find many things here of interest. But please do confine your wanderings to the house. The chapel, in particular, is in a state of great disrepair, and is not at all safe.
Jonathan	Very well.
Dracula	May I have the documents?
Jonathan	Of course.

Jonathan hands the briefcase to Dracula.

Dracula	Thank you, Mr Harker. I shall begin studying them immediately. You must be tired. Your room is at the top of the stairs. I hope you find it comfortable. Goodnight.

Dracula turns and walks to the back of the stage. Jonathan speaks to the audience.

Jonathan	I slept fitfully and woke late to a fine, clear day. I found food

waiting for me, ate, and then passed the time exploring the many rooms in the castle. But, almost from the moment of my waking, I was increasingly aware of a . . . strangeness about the place . . . a sense of decay and death . . . a rottenness within its very stones. In every room and passage, I found evidence of a history that reached far back into the past – a history once grand and noble, perhaps, but degenerate now, wasted, caving in upon its own lifeless sterility.

Dracula turns and comes forward. He speaks to Jonathan.

Dracula   My ancestors have lived here for many centuries. Long before the building of this castle they were a power in the land. A fierce, proud race, warrior-poets, defenders of their homeland against the forces of barbarism. They were true patriots, Mr Harker. They loved their country. They gave themselves to its rivers and forests and mountains, fed the very earth with their blood. And it grew rich and fertile with that blood. But now, the earth grows barren. The glories of the past crumble with the stones of this castle. The bones of my ancestors are dust in their tombs. I am the last of their line. In me alone they have life. And there are times I grow weary.

Jonathan speaks to the audience.

Jonathan   It was the next evening. As the sun set the Count arrived. I ate the food he brought me – though he did not eat. And we

talked in the great hall, by the light of a fire that cast crooked shadows across the cobwebbed walls.

Dracula	*[Continuing his explanation]* This is the reason I have made the decision to come to your country. There is nothing here for me now. Only the past. And one must look to the future, always.

Jonathan turns to Dracula.

Jonathan	Have you studied the documents?
Dracula	Yes. Everything appears to be in order.
Jonathan	And the property?
Dracula	It is excellent! I could desire none better.
Jonathan	There's nothing you wish to discuss?
Dracula	No. My good friend, Mr Hawkins, has been most thorough and meticulous. As, I'm sure, has been his assistant. He has written to me, and speaks of you highly.
Jonathan	It's very good of him. You're ready to sign, then?
Dracula	No. Not yet.
Jonathan	But you said everything was in order.
Dracula	Indeed it is.
Jonathan	Then may I ask the reason for your not signing?
Dracula	Yes. It is because I do not wish to. When I have completed all my preparations for leaving, then I will sign. It will be my last act here.
Jonathan	I see.
Dracula	Is it difficult?
Jonathan	I was rather hoping to have our business concluded tonight, and begin my journey home tomorrow.
Dracula	Then I am sorry to disappoint you. Is it so urgent you return?

Jonathan	Not urgent, but ... desirable ... to me.
Dracula	But it is desirable to me that you stay. For a few days only. I rarely have guests, Mr Harker, and it is a novelty of which I am loathe to be deprived. A few days, until my preparations are complete. Then you may go. Humour me in this, please. Say you will agree.
Jonathan	You appear to have left me no choice.
Dracula	Is it your heart that draws you home again, Mr Harker? Your heart and your loved one?
Jonathan	What?
Dracula	I found this among your papers.

*He takes a photograph from his pocket and hands it to **Jonathan**.*

Dracula	Your wife?
Jonathan	My fiancée ...
Dracula	She is very beautiful. Such fine, strong features. There is a nobility about her, a strength and depth of character. She is proud, yes?
Jonathan	I wouldn't say proud –
Dracula	You are a lucky man. Do not be concerned. You shall see her again before long. Until then, remain my guest.

*Dracula turns and goes. **Jonathan** speaks to the audience.*

Jonathan	I looked at the photograph of Mina, the woman who was to be my wife. And it was as if I was seeing her for the first time. Seeing her as he had seen her. There was something about the way he'd looked at her, a kind of ... hunger in his eyes. And suddenly, I felt the great distance that lay between us, a distance that seemed to be drawing me away from her. And suddenly too, I was unaccountably afraid.

Jonathan goes.

ACT 1 SCENE 1

SCENE 2

Mina enters and speaks to the audience.

Mina   It was a few weeks after Jonathan left that I went to Whitby to stay with Lucy. We'd been friends since childhood, and had written to each other regularly since Lucy had gone to live there. I was so looking forward to seeing her. Especially as, since Jonathan's leaving, I had experienced an increasing sense of . . . unease and anxiety, which came to me in strange, disturbing dreams. Dreams I could not remember on waking . . . except that, in all of them, there was a shadow, a formless shadow that seemed to be reaching out towards me.

Lucy enters and speaks to Mina.

Lucy   *[Laughing]* And since when have you paid any attention to dreams, Mina?

Mina   *[Turning to Lucy]* I don't, Lucy, not really . . .

Lucy   You poor thing. It's only that you're missing Jonathan.

Mina   Yes, I know.

Lucy   And it won't be long before he's home again, will it?

Mina	No . . .
Lucy	There you are, then. Dreams are nothing but . . . dreams. Nothing to be gloomy about.
Mina	Am I gloomy? I'm sorry, I don't mean to be. I'll try and be more cheerful.
Lucy	Good. Because I have some cheerful news. Some very cheerful news indeed.

Mina turns and speaks to the audience.

Mina	I'd known she had something to tell me ever since she met me at the station. Lucy was never very good at keeping her heart a secret. My . . . subdued manner had prevented her from telling me straightaway. But now that telling was to be delayed no longer.
Lucy	I wonder if you can guess?
Mina	*[Turning to Lucy]* I'd rather you told me.
Lucy	And I'd rather you guess. Can't you guess? Please. Look at me, Mina. Can't you?

Mina looks hard at Lucy. Then she speaks to the audience.

Mina	Then I saw the truth of it. What it was that made her eyes shine so, that had deepened the colour in her face, that lent a brightness to her whole being – I saw what it was that she'd been bursting to tell me ever since she'd met me at the station. She'd had a proposal of marriage.
Lucy	No. You're wrong.
Mina	*[Back to Lucy]* Oh – I was sure –
Lucy	Not one proposal. Three!

Mina speaks again to the audience.

Mina	Of course, only Lucy could have had three proposals. And, of course, she could not rest, now, until she'd described each of her suitors in great detail.

Lucy	First of all, there's Doctor Seward. He would just do for you, Mina, if you weren't already engaged to Jonathan. Although he's only 29, he's in charge of a large asylum in the town. I only made his acquaintance a short while ago, and had no idea of the depth of his feelings for me, until he came to see me the other day.
	Dr John Seward enters in a flashback scene, and speaks to the audience as if he is speaking to **Lucy**. *Throughout,* **Lucy** *speaks to* **Mina**.
Seward	Lucy – there's something I must speak to you about. I will come straight to the point – it concerns the manner in which … I have come to regard you …
Lucy	Poor man. He was trying to be so cool and composed, and yet I could tell how nervous he was. It quite made my heart ache for him.
Seward	Though I have known you but a brief while, Lucy, you have become dear to me – very dear. And I hope that I may also have become dear to you. So dear, in fact, that you might wish … to share your life with me.
Lucy	Of course, I told him that I could not. Not because of any ill-feeling towards him, but because my heart belonged to another.
Mina	Another?
Seward	Another? *[Holding up his hand as if to silence her]* There's no need to apologize. I understand. I'm sorry to have troubled you.
Lucy	Then he took my hands so tenderly in his and spoke with kindness and, I believe, complete sincerity.
Seward	*[Turning to Lucy]* I hope you will be happy with the man you have chosen. And if ever you find yourself in need of a friend, you must count on me as one of your best.
	Seward turns, and walks to the back of the stage. **Mina** *speaks to* **Lucy**.

Mina	Poor Doctor Seward. Now, who is the second?
Lucy	The second is a man with the delightful name of Quincey Morris.
	*Quincey Morris enters in another flashback scene and introduces himself. He has a slight American accent. Once again, he speaks to the audience as if he is speaking to **Lucy**, while **Lucy** speaks to **Mina**.*
Morris	Quincey P. Morris.
Lucy	He's an American – though he's lived so long in this country that he's lost all but a trace of his accent.
Morris	A good friend of John Seward – and Arthur Holmwood, whom I believe you also know.
Lucy	And on many evenings he amused us all with his stories and – tall tales.
Morris	For I've travelled the world, Miss Lucy, and I've been in places and seen such things that folks here in safe little England would never even dream of.
Lucy	But then, one of those evenings, being alone with me, he made his quite unexpected proposal.
Morris	Travelled the world, I have, and there's nothing I like better – but I'd be willing to hang up my boots and settle for a warm fire in a little country house, if I thought I'd be sharing that fire and that house with the one who means most to me. I mean you, Lucy.
Lucy	And, once again, I said that I couldn't accept such an offer, because my heart was given to someone else.
Mina	Someone else again? Who is this someone else?
Lucy	Be patient. You'll hear.
Morris	[*Turning to **Lucy***] Lucy, I have to tell you I'm disappointed. Mighty disappointed. I had thought the two of us – I thought we got on tolerably well – well enough in fact to … but it

seems I was mistaken. But you've been honest with me, Lucy. Honest and direct, and I thank you for that. And though you might not have found a husband in me, you've found yourself a true friend, and one who'll never let you down, whatever kind of fix you're in. I thank you again, and take my leave.

Morris turns and walks to the back of the stage.

Lucy	And he was gone, and he'd been so sweet that my heart felt like breaking, and I wept. I wept, Mina.
Mina	I'm sure you did, Lucy.
Lucy	And it was while I was still weeping that another man came into the room.

Arthur Holmwood enters in a third flashback scene and again he speaks to the audience as if he is speaking to Lucy. Lucy continues to speak to Mina.

Holmwood	Lucy.
Lucy	Arthur Holmwood, only son of Lord Godalming. I've not told you of him before, Mina. I've not told you how from the moment we first met he won my heart. I had never told him how I felt. And until that night, he had never confessed any feeling to me.
Holmwood	But now I do. And I ask if you would do me the greatest honour, and become my wife.
Mina	And this time you said yes?
Lucy	This time I said yes.
Holmwood	And made me the happiest of men. *[Turning and speaking to Lucy]* I'm afraid I must leave you for a little while to return home. My father is not well. But when he is better, and when I return, then we shall be married.

Holmwood turns and walks to the back of the stage.

Mina	So, it's to be Arthur Holmwood, then.
Lucy	Yes. It could be no other. But Mina – Doctor Seward and Mr

	Morris are so ... so sweet ... and I do have some affection for them ...
Mina	Of course you do.
Lucy	And though I do love Arthur ... I sometimes wonder why it is a woman must choose only one man to be her husband –
Mina	Lucy!
Lucy	Have I shocked you, Mina? Do you think I'm wicked? I can't help what I think –
Mina	No. I don't think you're wicked. But I do think you should be satisfied with one husband – as I will be with Jonathan.
Lucy	Yes, you're right of course. *[Impulsively]* Perhaps we can make it a double wedding, Mina. Me and Arthur, and you and Jonathan, when he returns from abroad. That would crown my happiness. I'm sure I don't know what I've done to deserve such happiness. All I can do is to thank God for sending me such a husband, and such good, true, and dear friends.

Lucy and Mina go. Seward, Morris, and Holmwood come forward and speak to the audience.

Seward	But though we were good and true friends –
Morris	Though we kept her in our hearts and thoughts –
Holmwood	And loved her more than anything –
Seward	We were powerless to help her –
Morris	God was powerless to help her –
Holmwood	The time when the evil came.

Seward, Morris, and Holmwood go.

● ●

SCENE 3

Jonathan enters and speaks to the audience.

Jonathan	The fear I had felt that night did not leave me. Although

Count Dracula continued to treat me with courtesy, there was something in his manner that hinted at some dark purpose, some shadow in his voice beneath his words that filled me with increasing dread. And, as time passed, it came to me that I was being kept prisoner in his castle, though for what reason I could not guess. And then, one night, my fears took on form and shape and stood before me, and I saw them in their true horror.

He pauses, collecting himself, as if he has to face the terror he felt that night again.

*As **Jonathan** continues his story, three **hags** enter slowly. They are dressed in ragged robes, with hoods covering their faces. They take up positions on three sides of the stage.*

Jonathan   I woke suddenly. It was still dark. I couldn't tell the time. Neither late nor early. A kind of . . . 'no-time'. . . where all time had ceased. Bright moonlight flooded the room, transforming it. Everything sharper, clearer, yet somehow unreal. As if I had stepped through a mirror into a world utterly different. I noticed first a sweet, rich smell in the air, a sickly perfume that was almost visible. And then – voices. I heard voices singing, soft at first, but growing stronger, a song without words, so beautiful . . . so fearful . . . a song of longing and desire . . . and despair . . . And with the song there came a mist. It drifted about the room, and glowed with a pale light, and there were shadows in the mist, shadows which took shape and form, and stepped out of the mist and stood before me.

*Jonathan turns, and faces the three **hags**. Their hands are claws. Their harsh voices have a hypnotic effect on **Jonathan**, paralyzing him. As they speak, they close in on him.*

Hag 1   From black chasms we come.

Hag 2   From earth's deep, from hell's pit.

Hag 3   From night's throat we come.

Hag 1   Listen to us.

Hag 2	Be still.
Hag 3	Listen. Hear our voice.
Hag 1	It is the scratch of the rat in the dry tomb.
Hag 2	The scratch of the spider's leg over the floor.
Hag 3	The scratch of the bat's wing in the hollow cave.
Hag 1	Do not move.
Hag 2	Do not stir.
Hag 3	Be still. You cannot move.
Hag 1	We are the death that cannot die.
Hag 2	We are the heart that cannot beat.
Hag 3	We are the soul that cannot fly.
Hag 1	We are hunger.
Hag 2	We are all that hungers under the cold moon.
Hag 3	We are hunger and you are our prey.
Hag 1	And already you are dead.
Hag 2	Already we feed.
Hag 3	Claws tear, teeth rip.
Hag 1	We suck the hot blood from your veins.
Hag 2	We suck the rich life from your limbs.
Hag 3	We suck the last breath from your soul.
Hag 1	We are the children of the night.
Hag 2	The wolf's howl.
Hag 3	The owl's shriek.
Hag 1	We are hunger.
Hag 2	We are all the hungers under the cold moon.

Hag 3	We are hunger, and you are our prey.
	*The **hags** have completely encircled **Jonathan** now, and are about to take hold of him when **Dracula** enters.*
Dracula	Leave him!
	*The **hags** fall back from **Jonathan**.*
	How dare you touch him! This man is not for you. Do you hear me? Leave him, I say. He belongs to me.
Hag 1	What then for us?
Hag 2	Where do we feed?
Hag 3	Is there nothing for us?
Dracula	Feed where you will. The child in its cot. The old woman by her fire. The priest at his prayers. All are for your taking, except him.
Hag 1	You are our master.
Hag 2	You made us, we are yours.
Hag 3	*[Demanding eagerly]* A gift for your creatures!
All Hags	A gift! A gift!
Dracula	You think I would forget my children? Outside there is something. It lives. It kicks. Its life is young, its blood new-born. Go. Take it. Feast well.
Hag 1	A child!
Hag 2	A human child!
Hag 3	He gives us life.
Hag 1	He gives us blood.
Hag 2	Come, sisters. We go.
Hag 3	We go to feed.
	*The **hags** go. **Dracula** approaches **Jonathan**.*

Dracula	You think this is a dream, Mr Harker? A terrible dream from which you will wake? I tell you, it is no dream, and you shall not wake. Your world is the dream, this world the reality. The world of night, which I have made. And soon, very soon, that world will engulf you, and you shall dwell in its darkness forever. You – and she who has your heart. You belong to me, Mr Harker, and so does she. And I shall feed upon you both. You first, then her. And it is you, you who send me to her. You give her to me. Know this, Mr Harker. Know it – and despair.

Dracula goes. Jonathan speaks to the audience.

Jonathan	I woke the next morning from horror into horror. The light of day brought with it no comfort. I was locked within my room, a captive, and prey to a . . . a monster that fed on human blood. My only hope lay in escape, and throughout that day, and the night that followed, I formulated a plan.

I had deduced that the Count walked abroad only through the hours of darkness and that, if I were to attempt an escape, it must be while the sun shone. But the next morning, I saw a cart arrive, driven by four men. And these four men carried a number of heavy wooden boxes from the chapel and loaded them onto the cart. It was not until late afternoon that the cart finally left, and I knew that I must act immediately. So I climbed out of the window, and made my way along its ledge. Then, I crossed to the next ledge, and the next, and so on, until I stood above the chapel. From there I leaped down onto its roof. There was a hole in the roof, and looking down, I saw several coffins. I dropped down through the hole, and stood before one of them. The lid wasn't fixed down, but lay loose on top. I took hold of the lid, and lifted it away. And there, in the coffin, lay the Count! Neither dead nor alive, eye open and glassy, lips red with blood. In terror and disgust I turned away. My only thought was to flee from that terrible place. To flee from the place of death and doom.

Jonathan goes.

SCENE 4

*Mina enters and speaks to the audience. As she speaks, **Lucy** enters and stands by her, followed by **Mr Swales** who sits down on the bench seat. **Mr Swales** speaks with a Yorkshire accent.*

Mina After a while, the letters from Jonathan stopped coming. One week passed, a second week, and I heard nothing from him. I told myself that he was in a remote part of the world, that his duties would occupy much of his time, that there were any number of reasons why I should not hear from him – yet I could not dispel the feeling of unease that grew daily within me. But I did my best to allay my fears, and to pass my time pleasantly with Lucy, who was happier than I'd ever known her. And she seemed happiest of all when we walked together in the churchyard behind the old abbey, which stood on a headland looking down upon the harbour, and out across the sea.

*Lucy introduces **Mina** to Mr Swales.*

Lucy   Mina, this is Mr Swales. Our town's oldest inhabitant, so they say.

Mr Swales   And how would you know my name and my age, miss?

Lucy   My mother's told me all about you. *[To **Mina**]* Mr Swales claims to be nearly a hundred years old.

Mina   Is that so, Mr Swales?

Mr Swales   I do claim it when folk ask – though you must never believe all you're told.

Lucy   He's known as something of an oracle, aren't you, Mr Swales?

Mr Swales   If you mean I've knocked around long enough to have seen summat of the world and its ways, I won't disagree with you.

Mina   Perhaps you could tell me something, then, Mr Swales. I have heard it said that, whenever a ship is lost at sea, a phantom bell tolls out in the harbour.

Mr Swales   Aye, I've heard it said as well. And no doubt you've also heard it said there's a ghost haunts the old abbey.

Mina   That's right, yes! The White Lady! She appears from time to time at one of the empty windows. So I've been told.

Lucy   Usually at dusk, and with a look of sorrow and loss on her face. They say she died for love.

Mina   A delightfully chilling tale.

Mr Swales   That's as maybe. I've also heard it said – and by men and women with more education than me – that come the Last Day the dead will rise up out of their graves, and be as they were in life. But I don't put no more credence to that, neither, nor any such children's fancies.

Lucy   Mr Swales! You're an unbeliever!

Mr Swales   Miss, I've been on this earth a good few years, and in that time I've travelled across most of it, man and boy, aboard fishers

37

and whalers. And if I've learned owt, it's to believe only what I see with my own eyes – and even then to doubt it.

Mina   I bow to your superior experience, Mr Swales. But do you really not believe in anything beyond our mere mortal existence?

Mr Swales   Do I believe in ghosts and such like? No, miss, I don't. The dead are so much dust and mould. Take these that are buried in this churchyard here. I've come to sit in this place for more years than I care to remember, and I've not heard one of them so much as sneeze, let alone seen one get out of his grave and walk.

Mina turns and speaks to the audience.

Mina   So we passed the summer, and many times had occasion to talk with Mr Swales. And the last such occasion was that evening in August, before the night of the storm.

Lucy   I think the weather will break soon.

Mr Swales   Aye, it will that, miss. And break with a vengeance if I'm not mistook.

Mina   *[Turning back to Lucy and Mr Swales]* It will bring us some relief, I hope. These last days have been so hot and oppressive.

Mr Swales   Let's just hope that's all it brings, miss, and nowt else.

Lucy   What do you mean, Mr Swales?

Mr Swales   To be honest, I don't rightly know what I mean. Call it a feeling. There's summat coming with this storm. What it might be, I can't say. Though I sense there's nowt good about it.

Mina   This isn't like you, Mr Swales. You sound almost . . . superstitious.

Mr Swales   Maybe it's just that I can feel my own death approaching.

Lucy   Surely not! You're hale and hearty yet!

Mr Swales	I've walked this earth a long time, miss, and I can't be expected to walk it forever.
Mina	I refuse to believe it, Mr Swales. You'll live to be a hundred, I'm sure.
Mr Swales	Maybe, and maybe not. Who can tell when death will come to us? Maybe it's when we're looking for it, and maybe it's not. But whenever it comes, and whatever form it takes, I pray I may meet it grinning.

Mina turns and speaks to the audience.

Mina	We left him there, on his seat, and returned to Lucy's home. And I wish I'd turned round and looked upon him once more, and raised my hand in farewell, for after that evening, I never saw him in the world again.

Mina and Lucy go. Mr Swales speaks to the audience.

Mr Swales	I watched them go, and there were more I wanted to say to them, but I couldn't find the words. I wanted to warn them, but I didn't know of what. Bolt your doors, seal your windows tight, for there's summat coming, out there over the North Sea, riding high and proud on the back of the storm, something wicked in the wind and the shivering light. And though I can't see its face, it smells like death. Aye, I should've told those things, but I didn't, and never had the chance again. For that night I saw its face, and they found me the next day with my neck broke and my heart burst. So evil came into this land, and cast its shadow upon it, and took possession.

The lights fade to blackout.

SCENE 1

*The lights rise. The **newspaper reporter** enters and speaks to the audience.*

Reporter   Yesterday's sudden and violent storm was perhaps the most ferocious to have erupted on the town within living memory. This fact alone would warrant its inclusion in this newspaper. Yet it also brought with it events so strange and unique that they will be imprinted on the town's memory for a long time to come. The most noteworthy of these was the appearance of a ship at the height of the storm, with all sails set, making for the harbour, and caught in the very teeth of the gale. Despite the howling winds and driving rain, many townsfolk gathered at the harbour side to watch with baited breath and anxious hearts as the ship was tossed this way and that on the heaving ocean, several times disappearing completely from sight beneath the onslaught of the waves, only to reappear again, to the cheers of the gathered crowd. Against all apparent odds, the ship weathered the storm, and at last drew into the harbour, where the townsfolk prepared to greet and congratulate the gallant crew – until it was discovered that but for one man, there was no crew aboard – and that one was a corpse tied to the ship's wheel. A great awe came on all as they realized that the ship had found harbour unsteered save by the hand of a dead man!

The coastguard enters and speaks to the audience.

Coastguard As coastguard, I was first on board the vessel. She was Russian, a merchantman. Her name, the Demeter. What became of her crew, God alone will ever know. As for the poor fellow at the ship's wheel, some desperate need must have driven him to lash himself there. The rope had cut through his flesh to the bone, and there was a crucifix clutched in his right hand. The doctor later confirmed that he'd been dead for two days, but could find no definite cause of death – except perhaps fear. For there was a look on his face of … sheer terror and horror … a look, I confess, that chilled me to the bone. As for the ship's cargo, all I found in the hold were several wooden boxes, about six feet in length, and these contained nothing but mouldering earth. The whole thing is a mystery, and a damned unpleasant one at that, and as far as I can tell shall probably remain so.

The coastguard goes. The reporter also turns to leave, then stops and turns back to the audience.

Reporter There was one more unusual event worthy of mention in this journal. Shortly after the ship came into harbour, a large, grey dog was seen by many, including this reporter, to leap off the deck onto the quayside, and then to make its way along the path to the clifftop where the churchyard stands. But what the dog was doing on board the ship, and what became of it thereafter no one knows, for to date it has not been seen again.

The reporter goes.

SCENE 2

Immediately, Renfield, a patient at Dr Seward's asylum, enters. He looks unkempt and seems agitated. He cries out, wildly.

| Renfield | My master! My master has come! He is here! Master! Hear me! I'm waiting! I'm ready to do your bidding, Master! |

Bennett and Withers enter. They are attendants at the asylum. Bennett carries a cudgel.

| Bennett | What's all this noise about, Renfield? |
| Withers | Keep it down. |

Renfield turns to them.

Renfield	He's here. At last! He's come with the storm! He summoned it and it brought him!
Bennett	Who are you talking about?
Renfield	My master.
Withers	Oh, yes? And who might your master be, Renfield?
Bennett	Old Nick, most likely.
Withers	Or Old King Cole.
Renfield	I've waited for him a long time. I have been faithful. He knows I have. And he will reward me for my faithfulness.
Bennett	You're going to get a reward, are you?
Renfield	Oh, yes. He promised I would.
Withers	And what might that reward be?
Renfield	Life. Eternal life.
Bennett	His master must be God Almighty, then.
Withers	Or like I said, the Devil.

Renfield starts to chant.

| Renfield | Life is blood and blood is life. Life is blood and blood is life. Life is blood and blood is life . . . |

He continues chanting as Bennett and Withers speak.

| Bennett | There he goes again. |

Withers	Shut it, will you, Renfield?
Renfield	Life is blood and blood is life, life is blood and blood is life ...
Bennett	Gets on my nerves, that does.
Withers	Mine, too. That's enough, I said!
	Renfield's chanting grows louder and more agitated.
Renfield	Life is blood and blood is life, life is blood and blood is life, life is blood and blood is life ...
Bennett	Give us a break from it!
Withers	Shut it or I'll shut it for you!
	*Renfield cries out and attacks **Withers**, scratching his face.*
Renfield	Life is blood!
	***Withers** cries out.*
Bennett	You –
	***Bennett** hits **Renfield** with the cudgel, knocking him down. At that moment, **Seward** enters.*
Seward	What's going on? Bennett! Stop that!
Bennett	He attacked Withers, Doctor Seward.
Withers	Scratched my face with those nails of his. Look! He's drawn blood.
Bennett	Went wild, he did.
Seward	Even so, I've told you before we are not to use violence against our patients.
Withers	Even if they use violence against us?
Seward	That is what marks the difference between them and us, Mr Withers.
	Renfield squats on the floor, sucking and licking his fingers. Seward approaches him.

Seward	He appears calm enough, now.
Bennett	Don't let that fool you, Doctor Seward. There's murder in his heart, sure enough. Cut all our throats if he could.
Seward	Renfield. Renfield. What are you doing?
Renfield	Blood. Life is blood.
Withers	Oh, God. He's licking my blood off his fingers.
Bennett	He's an animal. That's what he is.
Seward	No, Mr Bennett. He's not. I'm afraid he's all too human, and that's the tragedy of it. You can both go, now. I'll stay with him for a while.
Withers	You be careful, Doctor Seward. This storm's got him all wound up. He's drawn blood, and given the chance he's likely to do it again.
Seward	I'll take care.
Bennett	We won't be far if you need us.

Withers and Bennett go. Renfield remains squatting on the floor. Seward speaks to the audience.

Seward	After my disappointment in the matter concerning Miss Lucy Westenra – soon to become Mrs Lucy Holmwood – I devoted myself even more entirely to my work here at the asylum. I became intrigued by the case of one particular patient – Renfield. His madness showed itself in a most singular obsession, which I discovered some time ago, upon one of my first visits to him.

The following action takes place in flashback.

Renfield begins to move about the floor, as if hunting something. Then, he reaches out suddenly, and snatches something up, cupping it in his fist, and hugging it to himself with pleasure. Seward turns to him.

Seward	Renfield. What's that you have there?

Renfield	You can't have it! It's mine!
Seward	I don't want it, whatever it is. I simply want to know what it is. Show me, would you?

A little suspiciously, **Renfield** *stands and crosses to* **Seward**.

Renfield	Careful. It mustn't escape.

He holds his cupped fist up to **Seward's** *face and then opens it a little.*

Seward	A fly!

Renfield *closes his fist again.*

Renfield	One of many. Many. There shall be many.

He moves away from **Seward** *who continues to tell his story to the audience. As* **Seward** *speaks,* **Renfield** *takes a small box out of his pocket, and places the caught fly in it.*

Seward	He requested sugar to lay in small piles about his cell, which he used to attract the flies, and also a small box in which to keep them. I saw no reason to deny his requests. Indeed, I was eager for him to continue in his obsession, in order that I should observe it, and see in what direction it might lead.

Renfield *turns to* **Seward**, *holding up the box.*

Renfield	You hear them? Buzzing, buzzing. Fat flies, filled with life. The box is full. It can take no more.
Seward	What will you do with them?
Renfield	You'll see. Wait! Hold this! Don't let them out!

Renfield *gives the box to* **Seward**, *drops to his knees, and hunts again. Once more, he makes a grab at something, and cups it in his fist. He stands, triumphant, and turns to* **Seward**.

	There! Now we can move on!
Seward	What's that? Another fly?

Renfield	No. It isn't flies I want, now. It's spiders. I have a spider! And he shall feast well, and grow fat!

Renfield takes the box from Seward, and places the spider in it.

One spider, and another, and another. Soon, no more flies, and a box full of spiders. Fat spiders. Do you see?

He turns from Seward, drops to the floor, and begins hunting spiders, snatching them up and placing them in the box. Seward speaks again to the audience.

Seward	Needless to say, I did not. But daily I observed him gripped in the mania of this new obsession – as eager almost as he was to follow it through to its ultimate end.
Renfield	Life is blood and blood is life.
Seward	*[Turning to Renfield]* What? What's that you say?
Renfield	Life is blood and blood is life. Spiders eat flies and birds eat spiders. And here's a whole boxful! A boxful of spiders for a bird to feed on. And he will grow so fat, so fat and full of blood and life.

He turns from Seward and sits on the floor with his back to the audience. Seward turns back to the audience and continues his story.

Seward	So at last I began to glimpse some reason and progression in his mania. From spiders he moved on to birds, luring several sparrows from outside into his room.

Bennett and Withers enter.

Bennett	And a right mess they've made of it as well.
Withers	Filth and droppings everywhere.
Bennett	You sure it's healthy to let him keep them in here, Doctor Seward?
Seward	I don't think there's any harm in it. They aren't that much of a nuisance at present. And it will be interesting to see what he intends to do with them.

Withers	I know what I'd like to do with them. Get rid of the whole lot and clean this place up. Clean him up as well, while I'm at it.
Seward	I'm sure it won't continue for much longer, Mr Withers. I've been observing each obsession of his and –
Bennett	*[Suddenly noticing **Renfield**]* Oh, my God! You animal! You filthy, stinking animal!

*As **Bennett** cries out, **Renfield** scuttles away, stuffing something into his mouth with his hands.*

Seward	Mr Bennett! What is it? What's wrong?
Bennett	Him! That's what's wrong! You see what he's doing? He's eating one of them blessed birds! Didn't even kill it! Just stuffed it into his mouth and he's eating it alive and raw!
Withers	No harm, eh, Doctor Seward? If you ask me, there's nothing but harm in that one. He's a creature full of harm and wickedness, if I've seen it in any living soul.
Bennett	Best get this place cleared of these birds, Doctor Seward. If you don't, he'll soon have it cleared for us.

***Bennett** and **Withers** go. **Renfield** sits, rocking himself backward and forward, and muttering over and over to himself. **Seward** speaks to the audience.*

Seward	After we took the birds away – to which he made most violent objection – he sank into a morbid, depressed state, uncommunicative except for his repeating over and over of his almost prayer-like chant.
Renfield	Life is blood and blood is life, life is blood and blood is life, life is blood and blood is life, life is blood –

***Renfield** stops suddenly and looks up. **Seward** continues to speak to the audience.*

Seward	Until the night of the storm.
Renfield	He's here. My master! He has come!
Seward	The night of madness and horror.

Renfield	He brings me freedom! He brings me life.
Seward	The night when evil came.

*Seward goes. **Renfield** stands, walks to the front, and speaks to the audience.*

Renfield	My master has come in the belly of the storm. My master is here, and he brings me blood!

Renfield goes.

● ●

SCENE 3

Mina enters and speaks to the audience.

Mina	The storm came but brought no break in the weather. The days that followed were hot and oppressive, almost unbearable. And with that oppressiveness, my concern for Jonathan's welfare increased. But not only for him. Since the storm, Lucy had become restless and distracted. She slept badly, and told me of strange, unsettling dreams that seemed to sap her energy. And she feared the coming of night, she said. She feared these dreams that haunted her. I thought that perhaps it was the terrible death of poor Mr Swales that had affected her. But then, one night, I saw that this was not so.

*During the following, **Lucy** enters behind **Mina**. She wears a shawl around her shoulders, held together by a brooch. She sits on the bench.*

Mina	I awoke myself from some dream to find Lucy's bed empty. The large window that faced out onto the garden was open. I rose and went out. There was dew on the grass, and I could see her footprints, leading across the garden and out. I followed them, and they led towards the ruins of the abbey. And there, in the distance, I saw her, on the bench where Mr Swales used to sit. But there was something strange about her. It was as if she was … waiting for something … or someone.

*As **Mina** speaks, **Dracula** enters and crosses to **Lucy**. He stands over her. His face is hidden from the audience. **Lucy** raises her head towards him.*

Mina	What I saw next made me think that I was still sleeping, still in the grip of some terrible dream. Out of the shadows a figure approached her, stood over her, and she raised her head towards him as if in greeting. The figure stooped over her, and she was lost in the darkness of his shadow. And I knew it was no dream, that it was real, for I gave a cry, and the figure turned its head towards me. In the light of the full moon, I saw its face. And it was the face of a beast.

Dracula turns suddenly to the audience. He is wearing the horrific mask of a wolf. He turns from Lucy and takes a step towards Mina. Then Lucy gives a sudden cry.

Lucy	No!

Dracula stops, turns back towards Lucy, then goes, quickly. Mina goes to Lucy, who looks at her, as if waking from a dream.

Mina? What's happening? What am I doing out here?

Mina	It's all right, Lucy. You've been sleepwalking, that's all.
Lucy	Sleepwalking?
Mina	Yes. I woke and found your bed empty. I followed you here.
Lucy	I've had the strangest dream ... so strange ... but I can't remember it ...

Mina	You're shivering. It's cold. Let me wrap your shawl more closely round you.

Mina readjusts Lucy's shawl around her shoulders and neck, fastening it with the brooch. As she does, Lucy gives a little cry of pain.

Mina	I'm sorry. I must have caught your neck with the pin. There. No harm done.
Lucy	Mina. I'm frightened.
Mina	Frightened? Of what?
Lucy	I don't know –
Mina	Don't be. I'm here. There's nothing to be frightened of. Nothing at all.

Mrs Westenra enters and speaks to the audience. As she does so, Mina sits with Lucy, holding her hand, stroking her hair, comforting her.

Mrs Westenra	In the days that followed, my daughter grew increasingly lethargic. I, of course, was much concerned for her welfare, but hoped that, with the care and attention of Mina and myself, she would soon recover her full health.
Mina	[To the audience] But she didn't. With each passing day, the energy and life seemed to be draining out of her body. Yet at night she could not sleep. Several times I woke to find her sitting up in bed, staring wildly about her, as if disturbed by some presence I could not perceive.
Lucy	A face at the window, red eyes gleaming. Something scratching at the glass. It wants to get in!
Mrs Westenra	[Approaching Lucy] It's only a dream, dear. Pay no heed to it. Dreams can't harm you.

Mrs Westenra speaks to Mina.

Mrs Westenra	It is only a dream, isn't it?
Mina	[Disconcerted] Of course. What else could it be?

Mrs Westenra	I don't know. I'm sure I don't know.
Mina	*[To the audience]* I told her nothing of what I'd seen that night in the churchyard. What could I tell her? For I hardly knew what it was myself.
Mrs Westenra	*[Turning back to the audience]* I wrote to Mr Holmwood and told him of Lucy's condition, and he replied by return of post to say that he would be with us within the week. I felt sure that his arrival would do something to revive Lucy.

Dracula enters and stands at the side of the stage. Lucy looks up suddenly and points towards him.

Lucy	*[Softly and urgently]* There! The same! The same face, the same red eyes!

Mina continues to tell her story to the audience.

Mina	We were sitting together in the churchyard one evening, when suddenly she spoke, her voice low and urgent.
Lucy	Do you see him, Mina? There!
Mina	I turned and saw the figure of a man, standing some way off. But the setting sun was behind him, and I could not see his face.
Lucy	Always the same.
Mina	*[Turning back to Lucy]* What do you mean, Lucy? Who is that man? Do you know him?
Lucy	No. At least . . . I don't know what I mean . . . it was like my dream . . . the dream I have every night . . .

Dracula goes.

Mina	Don't think of your dreams, Lucy. Think of the life you have. Think of Arthur. He'll be here soon, and then everything will be all right.
Mrs Westenra	*[To the audience]* And I was glad that he was coming. Being . . . not well myself, I don't know how I would have cared for

Lucy alone. Because shortly after, Mina told us she would have to leave.

*Mina stands and speaks to **Lucy** and **Mrs Westenra**.*

Mina   I've had news of Jonathan. A letter came today . . . from a hospital in Budapest. That's where he is. He's been ill, but he's recovering now. That's why I haven't heard from him these past weeks.

Mrs Westenra   Ill? Do they say in the letter what's wrong with him?

Mina   Not exactly. He appears to have had . . . some kind of breakdown . . .

Lucy   Oh, Mina!

Mina   You do see, don't you? I must go.

Mrs Westenra   Yes, Mina, of course you must.

Lucy   Jonathan needs you. Go to him. I'll be all right. Arthur will be here in a day or two. And, thanks to your care and your dear friendship, I am feeling much better. By the time you return, you'll see I'll be quite my old self again.

Mina   I'm certain you will, Lucy.

Lucy   You can depend upon it.

Mina speaks to the audience.

Mina   So I said farewell to Lucy, and left, eager to make the journey, but full of fear and apprehension as to what I might find at the end of it. I did not know that my journey was to be much longer than I thought, that it would take me to a world I did not know existed. And that what I found there would be like nothing I could ever imagine.

*Mina goes. **Mrs Westenra** sits beside **Lucy** on the bench. **Holmwood**, **Morris**, and **Seward** enter and stand separately on three areas of the stage, around **Lucy** and her mother, as if protecting them. They speak to the audience.*

Holmwood   And we could not imagine –

Morris	No one could ever imagine –
Seward	When we came to stay with her –
Holmwood	To love and protect her –
Morris	To be her guardians as we'd promised –
Seward	We could not imagine what world it was –
Holmwood	What world of shadow had fallen across ours –
Morris	And it had called to Lucy –
Seward	And she had entered it.

• •

SCENE 4

Professor Van Helsing enters and stands at the centre front of the stage. He speaks only to the audience.

Van Helsing   I was abroad when my former student, Doctor Seward, wrote to me concerning the girl's case. And though it intrigued me and I gave it my full attention, yet I did not fully realize the grave danger she was in. I wrote to him, suggesting certain courses of action that could be taken and, to be honest, put the matter to the back of my mind.

*During the following, **Holmwood, Morris,** and **Seward** speak to the audience.*

Holmwood   But despite these remedies, Lucy did not get better.

Morris   Her condition only seemed to grow worse.

Seward   And she grew weaker and paler every day, as if something were draining the blood from her body.

Lucy speaks to the audience, her voice flat, as in a dream.

Lucy   I lived my life between waking and dreaming, not knowing which was which, as if my soul were slowly being drawn from my body. My days were a mist that thickened about me, my nights were filled with fear that came with the scratching of claws at the glass. And once there was a sweetness in the room and the fear turned away, but then the sweetness was taken and the fear returned, and it was stronger than ever.

Van Helsing	The second letter I received from Doctor Seward informed me in more detail of her symptoms, the foremost of which was an extreme anaemia, with accompanying lethargy. Doctor Seward's concern for his patient was obvious and, while I could offer no explanation, I wrote back and suggested that she be given, without delay, a transfusion of blood, in an attempt to reverse, or at least arrest the illness.
Holmwood	But nothing worked. Nothing! No treatment or remedy!
Morris	It seemed we were all powerless to help her.
Seward	And the only outward sign of any infection, the two wounds on her neck that would not heal.
Van Helsing	*[Realizing the truth]* A wound to her neck! It was then, and only then, that the true nature of this 'illness' became clear to me. And the peril in which the girl's life and soul stood. I wrote back immediately, saying that I would come there myself. In the meantime, her room was to be hung with flowers of wild garlic – the door and windows especially – and that these should on no account be moved. I would explain all, I said, when I arrived.

Van Helsing goes.

Holmwood	Flowers of garlic? Is this medical science or peasant superstition?

Holmwood turns his back to Lucy.

Morris	Despite our doubts we did as Professor Van Helsing had instructed.

Morris turns his back to Lucy.

Seward	Because, quite frankly, I was at a loss, and there seemed nothing else that we could do.

Seward turns his back to Lucy. Holmwood, Morris, and Seward remain in their positions throughout the following. Lucy speaks to herself as if in a dream. As she does so, she moves to draw back the curtain to reveal the French window. She remains there, gazing outside.

Lucy

Nothing they can do. Nothing to be done. See, the sun sets, the sky grows red, the earth grows dark. And out of the darkness and the redness in the west he comes, a mist creeping along the earth, cold fingers reaching towards my heart. Squeezing it, squeezing it tight. There, he stands at the window. There he waits to gain entrance. The same, always the same.

Mrs Westenra speaks to Lucy.

Mrs Westenra

What was that you said, Lucy?

Lucy

[Coming out of her dream] What, Mother? Did I speak?

Mrs Westenra

Yes.

Lucy

I don't know what I said. I don't remember. Nothing of importance.

Mrs Westenra

It's growing dark. Come away from the window, now. Get into bed.

Lucy moves back to sit on the bench, but continues to look towards the window.

Lucy

Not just yet. I want to sit here for a while and watch the sun set. It's so beautiful, isn't it, Mother?

Mrs Westenra

The sunset?

Lucy

The world, Mother. The world is so beautiful. I wish the dark wouldn't come to take it from us.

Mrs Westenra

The world is still there in the dark. It's only the light that's gone. Go to sleep. Then the light will return all the sooner.

Lucy

No, it won't. I fear the light will never come again.

Mrs Westenra

Lucy! What do you mean?

Lucy

[Turning back to her mother] Nothing.

Mrs Westenra	You make me afraid when you speak like that.
Lucy	I'm sorry. I'm just tired. I don't know what I'm saying.
Mrs Westenra	*[Caring and concerned]* Get into bed then –
Lucy	*[Sharply]* No! *[Softening her voice]* I will, soon. When the sun has set. You can leave me. I'll be quite all right.
Mrs Westenra	If you're sure –
Lucy	Go and sit with Arthur. Keep him company.
Mrs Westenra	He has company. Have you forgotten? Doctor Seward and Mr Morris are both here.
Lucy	Yes, of course. My three guardians. I'm very lucky, aren't I, Mother?
Mrs Westenra	Yes. You are. And I'm very lucky to have such a daughter as you.
Lucy	Kiss me goodnight.

Mrs Westenra kisses Lucy. Lucy holds her suddenly, very tight, then lets her go.

Lucy	Mother, when you see Arthur, will you tell him that I love him very much?
Mrs Westenra	You can tell him that yourself. Do you want him to come and see you?
Lucy	No. Please. Just tell him.
Mrs Westenra	All right. I will.
Lucy	Thank you. Goodnight now, Mother.
Mrs Westenra	Goodnight, dear.

Mrs Westenra goes. Lucy speaks to the audience.

Lucy	I turned back to look out of the window. The sun had almost set. A line of darkness was rising up into the sky from the horizon, deepening, spreading. And in the dark, a knot of blackness forming, hardening, tightening, my death

56

approaching. Coming like a ship on a blood-red sea, a ship with ragged, tattered sails, riding the waves of darkness. And a figure on the prow, leaning towards me, hungry and eager, urging the ship on. Then the waves rolled higher and higher, and they crashed about me, and all was drowned and my death was here.

Dracula enters through the French window, leaving it slightly open.

Dracula	Lucy. I have come for you at last.

Lucy stands in fear. Dracula holds out his hand to her.

Dracula	Come to me. Come willingly. You know you must.
Lucy	Where's my mother? I want my mother!
Dracula	She will not come. I showed her my face and it was too much. She's dead. Gone to hell with all her sins upon her.
Lucy	No!
Dracula	Why should you care about the dead? The dead mean nothing to such as you or I. They are so much dust and mould. We tower above them. We stride the world like giants. We are immortal. Soon you will know the taste of pure freedom, and there is none so sweet. One kiss. One last kiss is all.

Dracula walks towards Lucy, takes her hand, leans towards her and kisses her once, gently, on the neck. He steps back and lets go of her hand.

Dracula	There. It is done.

He turns to go.

Lucy	Where are you going?
Dracula	I must leave you now. But only for a little while. Not long, and you shall be with me.

Dracula goes. Lucy speaks to the audience.

Lucy	And he was gone, but the darkness remained. And my soul

wept ... but I did not hear it, for soon I too would walk in the dark world eternal.

Lucy goes.

• •

SCENE 5

Holmwood draws the curtain to cover the French window and then returns to his place.
Van Helsing enters and speaks to the audience.

Van Helsing So I came at last to a house of sorrow and mourning. But though I had failed the poor girl in her struggle with horror, yet I knew there was still work to be done. For I may have come too late to save her life, but not perhaps too late to save her soul.

Seward, Morris, and Holmwood turn to Van Helsing.
Seward introduces Van Helsing to his two friends.

Seward Arthur – Quincey – this is the man I told you of – Professor Van Helsing.

Van Helsing I am pleased to meet you both – though I wish the circumstances had been happier.

Morris So do we, Professor. And none more so than Arthur here.

Van Helsing Mr Holmwood – you were to have married the unfortunate young lady. My sincere condolences to you.

Holmwood Thank you. I wish – I wish you could have arrived sooner –

Van Helsing So do I.

Holmwood Perhaps you might have been able to save her.

Van Helsing Perhaps – and perhaps not. You were with her when she ... finally passed away?

Morris We all were.

Van Helsing Tell me what happened.

Holmwood What is there to tell? She died.

Van Helsing	Yes, but . . . if you could describe in detail the circumstances of her final moments . . .
Morris	*[Angry and upset]* What the hell for? What good would it do?
Van Helsing	It may help to prevent others from succumbing to the same . . . illness.
Seward	You think it may be something contagious?
Van Helsing	It may be. I cannot tell unless I have all the facts before me. Please.
Holmwood	I went in to see her early in the morning. She was lying on the floor and the window was open –
Van Helsing	Open? I gave instructions that it was to be kept shut at all times, especially during the night –
Seward	The window had been closed. I checked it myself before I went to bed.
Van Helsing	What of the garlic flowers I said should be hung from it?
Seward	Mrs Westenra removed them. The smell –
Van Helsing	That was a bad mistake.
Morris	If it was, Mrs Westenra paid a heavy price for it.
Van Helsing	Yes. She died as well. From heart failure, you said, John?
Seward	That's right. I found her in her own bedroom. The window was open there too.
Van Helsing	I see. Mr Holmwood, if you can find it in yourself to continue . . .
Holmwood	I put Lucy back into bed. I could see she was very weak. Her breathing was so shallow –
Van Helsing	Did she say anything?
Holmwood	No.
Van Helsing	Nothing?

Morris	She did try to speak. Just before the end –
Van Helsing	Did you hear what she said?
Morris	No. Her voice was too weak. Is it important?
Van Helsing	It may have been. Was her end peaceful?
Holmwood	*[Interrupting]* Yes, yes it was. Very peaceful. She passed as gently from this world, as she had lived in it.
Van Helsing	I am ... glad to hear it. And the marks on her neck? John, you wrote to me of two small wounds on her neck. Caused by the pin of a brooch, you said.
Seward	That's right. They weren't particularly serious – but they wouldn't heal.
Van Helsing	And were they still open when she died?
Seward	No. They appeared to have healed up entirely. In fact, there was no sign of them.
Van Helsing	And her features in death, they were peaceful?
Holmwood	I've already told you.
Van Helsing	May I see her?
Morris	She's in her coffin.
Van Helsing	Just for a moment.
Morris	It's been sealed.
Van Helsing	Nevertheless –
Holmwood	*[Very upset]* No! No, you may not see her! All these questions you're asking, what do they matter? What does any of this matter? She's dead! Nothing you can do will bring her back! Let her go to her rest. Let her be disturbed no more!

Holmwood storms out.

| Van Helsing | He's understandably upset. |
| Morris | We all are, Professor. |

Van Helsing	Of course, of course. Forgive my briskness, Mr Morris. It is not my intention to cause undue distress to the bereaved. However – *[Stopping]* No. We will talk no more. As Mr Holmwood said, let Miss Westenra be interred, and be at peace. And let us all pray for her soul.
Morris	I'll say amen to that.
	Morris turns to go, then stops, and turns back.
	One thing, Professor. When Arthur said she died peacefully – well . . . that wasn't quite the case.
Van Helsing	No?
Morris	Just before she died – at the moment of her death – something happened – a . . . change came over her.
Van Helsing	What kind of change?
Morris	Something in her face – a light in her eyes – something . . . savage – as if she had suddenly become possessed.
Van Helsing	And then?
Morris	Then it passed, as quickly as it came, and she died.
Van Helsing	Thank you for telling me, Mr Morris.
Morris	I thought I should. If it can shed any light on the cause of her death –
Van Helsing	It may shed a great light indeed.
Morris	Good. Because I told that girl I'd do anything for her, and even though she's gone from us, that still stands.
	Morris goes. Van Helsing speaks to Seward.
Van Helsing	John. What do you think killed her?
Seward	I confess I'm not certain. Loss of blood was certainly a factor.
Van Helsing	This continued throughout her illness, despite the transfusions you gave her?
Seward	Yes. It was baffling. A mystery.

Van Helsing	There is much that is mysterious about this business. And there is much that I fear may yet be revealed.
Seward	What do you mean?
Van Helsing	John, once the funeral is over, you and I shall go and talk together, in private. There are things I must tell you, things I have discovered, which I believe have a direct bearing on what has happened here. And if I am correct, we may still have work to do before the poor soul of Miss Westenra can finally be laid to rest.
Seward	*[Horrified]* What do you mean?
Van Helsing	Now is not the time. We shall talk later. Let us go and join the others.

Van Helsing and Seward go.

• •

SCENE 6

The reporter enters and speaks to the audience.

Reporter	There have occurred in recent days in the town, several incidents of children going missing from their homes. Three cases have so far been reported, and, in each case, the circumstances were strikingly similar. First of all, the three children all live in the same area of the town – that which lies close to the old abbey and the churchyard beyond. Second, while each child was happily missing for a period of one night only, and was discovered again the next morning, they were all found to be extremely weak and having a pale, almost emaciated appearance. And, in each case, the child spoke of being met by a young, beautiful woman, and taken by her for a walk. But none of the children can remember anything that happened after that, until the time they were recovered. Finally, and perhaps most disturbingly, on the neck of each child was a small wound, which appeared to have been inflicted by some wild animal. The public can rest assured that this newspaper will continue to report and investigate any further occurrences of these strange and unsettling events.

ANOTHER CHILD GOES MISSING!

*The **reporter** goes. A **child** enters on one side of the stage and speaks to the audience.*

Child — I was playing with my friends by the abbey. They went home when it started to get dark, but I stayed a bit longer because I like watching the fishing boats come in. After I'd watched them I turned round to go home, and that's when I saw the lady.

*Lucy enters on the opposite side of the stage and stands, watching the **child**.*

She was standing there, looking at me, and when I saw her she smiled and spoke to me.

Lucy — *[To the **child**]* Do you want to go for a walk?

Child — *[To **Lucy**]* It's getting dark.

Lucy — You're not afraid of the dark, are you?

Child — No ...

Lucy — Then come for a walk with me.

Child — *[To the audience]* She was very beautiful and she had a nice voice, and she walked towards me and held out her hand.

Lucy — *[Approaching the **child**, holding out her hand]* I don't like walking alone. Come and keep me company.

Child — *[To **Lucy**]* Where will we go?

Lucy — Not far. Just for a walk. A little walk. Come. Take my hand.

*The **child** takes **Lucy**'s hand, then turns to speak to the audience.*

| Child | So I did, and she took me through the abbey and into the churchyard. And while we were walking she kept singing to herself. Only I can't remember what the song was. And I can't remember anything else either. I can't remember anything else at all. |

Lucy and the child make their way to the seat.

Lucy	Here we are.
Child	Where?
Lucy	Here. I like it here, don't you? Among the dead. It's so peaceful.
Child	It's dark –
Lucy	Yes. I like the dark. Don't you like the dark?
Child	I ought to go home now –
Lucy	Why? Why do you want to go home? Don't go home. Stay with me. I'm lonely. I have no friends. Will you be my friend? Stay here with me and be my friend. You can sleep here, here on this bench. Sit down. Sit down here, and I'll put my arm around you and sing to you, and you can sleep. Sleep and dream such lovely dreams.

The child sits. Lucy sits next to him. She puts her arm around the child and sings, softly and gently. The child begins to fall asleep. On the far side of the stage, Van Helsing and Seward enter, watching secretly. Van Helsing carries a crucifix which he keeps hidden. They speak softly.

Van Helsing	There! You see?
Seward	It's her ... Lucy ...
Van Helsing	No. What you see is not Lucy. It is Nosferatu. The undead. You know now that what I told you is true.
Seward	Yes.
Van Helsing	Now! We must act quickly before she preys on this child.

*The **child** is asleep now. **Lucy** stands and lays him down gently. Then she bends over him, as if she intends to do him some harm. **Van Helsing** runs forward, crying out, and brandishing a crucifix.*

Van Helsing   Back! Back, evil one! Leave him!

*Lucy turns, savagely, and snarls and hisses like an animal at **Van Helsing**. She makes a threatening move towards him.*

Van Helsing   Back, I say! Leave this place! Away to your tomb!

*He thrusts the crucifix forwards. As if in pain, **Lucy** backs off stage, snarling and hissing. **Van Helsing** lowers the crucifix.*

Van Helsing   John. See to the child.

*Seward wakes the **child**.*

Child   *[Confused]* No – I want to go –

Seward   It's all right.

Child   Where's the lady?

Seward   She's gone. I'm a friend. There's nothing to be afraid of.

Van Helsing   *[To Seward]* I'll come to you later, at the asylum. Bring Mr Holmwood and Mr Morris there. It is time they too learned of this, and what it is we must do about it.

Seward   Very well. *[To the child]* How do you feel?

Child   Sleepy. What's been happening? I can't remember –

Seward   Don't worry. It doesn't matter. Come with me, now. I'll take you home.

*Seward and the **child** go. **Van Helsing** remains onstage.*

● ●

SCENE 7

Van Helsing speaks to the audience.

Van Helsing   I placed the crucifix at the entrance to the tomb, so keeping the creature from leaving and claiming more victims that night. Then, as we had arranged, I met with the others, and told them, as I had earlier told Doctor Seward, what I had learned myself over many years of that terrible creature of darkness and blood – the vampire.

Morris enters and speaks to the audience.

Morris	He told us how, from ancient times, there had been tales of those that lived on after death. Creatures of the dark whose souls were lost, whose existence was a death-in-life.

Holmwood enters and speaks to the audience.

Holmwood	How these undead could take on both human and animal form, and were, and are, known by many and varied names – the werewolf, the zombie, Nosferatu, the vampire.
Van Helsing	Having no soul, they have no humanity; they are beasts in human dress, driven only by appetite.
Morris	And that appetite is for human blood. They feed on the blood of the living. Blood sustains them and drives them. It is their only desire.
Holmwood	During the day they sleep in their graves and their tombs, for to be touched by the sun's light is fatal to them. The night is their time and it's then they walk the earth, immortal, seeking their victims in the hours of darkness.
Van Helsing	And once having found a victim, they prey on them, draining the blood from their body, and with each feeding their power over the victim grows. Until at last, death comes. But no ordinary death. For the power of the vampire has entered the victim's body, and they too become undead and immortal, and rise from their graves to feed upon others in turn.
Morris	And this, he said, is what had happened to Lucy.
Holmwood	Lucy had been the victim of a vampire.
Morris	And she, in turn, had become a vampire.
Holmwood	But I didn't believe it! I wouldn't!

Morris	Fairy tales! Horror stories!
Holmwood	How can we in our world believe such things?

Seward enters and speaks to the audience. He carries a small carpet bag.

Seward	And then I told them what I had seen that very night. How I had seen Lucy walking – or the monster that inhabited Lucy's body. I told them how, for all my belief in science and the powers of reason, I had been forced, through the evidence of my rational senses, to admit the existence of another power, and that there were such shadows in our world.

Van Helsing turns and speaks to the three men.

Van Helsing	Shadows, indeed, my friends. For while we may inhabit a world of light, there is also a world of darkness. Older than ours, perhaps, and often hidden from our more . . . enlightened eyes. But now that world has revealed itself to us, it has come upon ours, taken form and shape. And the form it walks in, at this present moment, is that of Miss Lucy Westenra. And we must act, act like heroes, with courage and strength, to drive it back to from where it came.

Seward hands Van Helsing the carpet bag.

Van Helsing	*[To Seward]* Is everything here as I instructed?
Seward	Yes.
Van Helsing	Then we are ready. And, with the coming of night, we must act.

Morris and Holmwood speak to the audience.

Morris	But still we found it hard to believe.
Holmwood	Even as we went that evening to Lucy's tomb, I refused to believe it.
Morris	As we stood there, waiting, as the sun set, I could accept nothing of what we'd been told.

Holmwood	Until the light died, and the shadows deepened, and the thing of darkness came walking from the tomb.

Lucy, as a vampire, enters talking to herself.

Lucy	I am hungry. Last night I did not feed. Something held me, a power, terrible. Now it is gone and I am free and I will feed.
Morris	My God! It is her!
Van Helsing	As I said. The dead do walk.
Seward	I thought you'd sealed her in.
Van Helsing	Last night I did. Today I removed the crucifix.
Seward	But why?
Van Helsing	So they could see what she has become.
Lucy	*[Looking towards the men]* I see them. Four. Three I know, one I do not. Waiting for me. I sense harm. But what can they do? What is their power against mine? Weak, frail they are. But with blood. Hot with blood.
Seward	She's seen us.
Morris	What do we do, Professor?
Van Helsing	Wait, for the moment. Let her come to us.
Lucy	*[Still talking to herself]* He is there. I see him looking. He sees her, his dearest one. With him I shall begin. His love shall deliver him to me.
Van Helsing	Whatever she does or says, do not approach her. She is hungry, and very dangerous.

*Lucy speaks, lovingly, to **Holmwood**.*

Lucy	Arthur? Arthur, is it you?
Holmwood	Lucy –
Van Helsing	Take care, Mr Holmwood.
Lucy	Arthur, my love. You have come for me at last.

Holmwood	Is it you?
Lucy	Yes. It is I, your own Lucy, your own true love.
Van Helsing	[To **Holmwood**] She is cunning. Do not be deceived by her.
Lucy	Come to me, Arthur. I'm not dead. I'm alive. You can see I am alive. Come. Hold me. I've been waiting for you, waiting for you to come to me.

*Lucy holds out her arms to **Holmwood**. He is drawn to her, almost against his will.*

Van Helsing	[Reaching out to restrain him] No, Mr Holmwood! Don't go to her!
Holmwood	Leave me –
Seward	It's not Lucy. It's a monster –

*Seward takes hold of **Holmwood** to hold him back. **Holmwood** flings him off.*

Holmwood	Let me go!

*As **Lucy** speaks, **Holmwood** moves slowly towards her.*

Lucy	That's right, Arthur. Come to me. Don't listen to them. They tell you lies. You can see it's me, your own, your very own. Come to me, now, and we shall never be parted again, we shall be together for all time!

*Holmwood is now within reach of **Lucy**. He holds out his arms to her.*

Holmwood	Lucy –

*With an animal snarl **Lucy** lunges at him, grabbing his wrists, pulling him with force and fury to her. **Holmwood** cries out in sudden fear. At the same moment, **Van Helsing** drops the carpet bag and springs forward, taking the crucifix from his pocket. He too grabs at **Holmwood** and pulls him from her grip.*

Van Helsing	[To **Lucy**] No, hell-hound! You shall not have him!

*Lucy turns on **Van Helsing**.*

Lucy	You, then!

Van Helsing thrusts the crucifix forward against Lucy's face. She screams in pain and terror, as if being horribly burned. She staggers back, clutching at her face. Van Helsing walks towards her, the crucifix held up, forcing her back with it, as she rages and snarls. Lucy goes, still snarling. Van Helsing lowers the crucifix.

Morris	Arthur? Are you OK?
Holmwood	Yes. Thank you. *[To Seward]* John, forgive me for how I acted.
Seward	There's nothing to forgive.
Holmwood	Professor –
Van Helsing	Say nothing, Mr Holmwood. You were severely tested tonight. And I think that now you must be tested even further.
Holmwood	In what way?
Van Helsing	You loved Lucy, did you not?
Holmwood	I still love her.
Van Helsing	Then help her to find peace. Free her soul from the monstrous shackles that bind it. Kill the beast within her. Do you have the strength of heart to do this?
Holmwood	I think so. I pray so.
Van Helsing	Good.

He picks up the carpet bag.

	Here I have the weapons of mercy. Let us go into the tomb, and do what must be done.

They all freeze except for Holmwood, who steps forward and speaks to the audience.

Holmwood	We entered the tomb. She was lying in her coffin. As I approached, I saw her eyes open, saw the savage light that flashed in them, the ferocious and pitiless hunger. She strove to rise but could not, pinned down by the power of the cross. I

knew now this was not Lucy. It was some evil thing that had fed on Lucy, and would feed on others, and go on feeding unless it was destroyed. I steeled myself to the task. I took up the weapons of mercy. I commended myself to God, and drove the wooden stake into her heart.

From offstage a sudden, loud, monstrous scream is heard, rising, then dying away to silence. **Morris, Seward,** *and* **Van Helsing** *speak to the audience.*

Morris   The beast howled in rage and pain, then fled into the darkness.

Seward   And she lay still and I could see by her face that she was at peace.

Van Helsing   And it was done. But it was not over.

The lights fade to blackout.

●●●

SCENE 1

*The lights rise. **Mina** enters and speaks to the audience.*

Mina   The hospital in Budapest where I found Jonathan was run by a religious order who cared for the sick. He had been found wandering on the outskirts of the city. Apart from exhaustion, there was nothing physically wrong with him. But mentally ... his mind had suffered some terrible shock that had left it almost broken. What had caused this shock the sisters could not tell, and I did not wish to know, not until he was recovered and ready to speak of it. So I nursed him back to health, and there in Budapest we were married, and then began our journey back to England.

***Jonathan** enters and speaks to the audience.*

Jonathan   And it was on that return voyage, that at last I found the courage, and the strength, to tell Mina all that I had experienced. But even then, I hesitated, for fear that she would not believe me, would think me mad ... for fear that, perhaps, I *was* mad ...

Mina   And indeed, when he first told me ... I did not know what to think. I could not bring myself to believe that such evil existed in our world. It was only when I learned that Lucy – and her mother – were dead, that I began to perceive some possible connection.

***Van Helsing** enters and speaks to the audience.*

Van Helsing   So they travelled to Whitby and met with Mr Holmwood and Doctor Seward, who told them the circumstances surrounding the girl's death. And at Doctor Seward's suggestion, they met with me, and I too heard Mr Harker's story.

Mina   Poor Jonathan. When he spoke of his ordeal, when he described the terrible things he had suffered, I could see how the horror of it lived in him again. I knew the pain it caused him, I felt that pain myself, and would have saved him from it if I could. But instead I urged him on, for I knew it was vital to us all, that his story must be told to the end.

Jonathan turns and speaks to Van Helsing.

Jonathan	I could not have done so without Mina. It was she who gave me the strength ...
Van Helsing	It was good that you found such strength, Mr Harker. Your wife's instincts were correct. I believe there is a connection between your experiences, and her friend's death. A very strong connection. *[To Mina]* What your husband has told me – and what you yourself have told of Lucy's illness – they explain much. Things begin to fall into place, and the mystery is not so obscure.
Mina	You believe it was Count Dracula who killed Lucy?
Van Helsing	I am almost certain of it. But before we can be sure, there are more facts we have to ascertain. What did Doctor Seward tell you of Lucy's death?
Mina	Not everything, I'm certain. Mr Holmwood was with us, and I think he was afraid of distressing him.
Van Helsing	Speak to Doctor Seward again. Ask him to tell you everything. You will find it distressing. But I think too you will understand more about this business. Mr Harker, I would like you to see what you can find out about Carfax Manor, and if anyone has taken residence there in recent times.
Jonathan	Of course.
Van Helsing	I myself must go to London. There is a man I know of who is an expert in European genealogies. I hope from him to find out more about this Count Dracula. I shall return by tomorrow evening. Then we shall all meet, and lay out the facts before us. And then we may be able to see how we are to act in the face of this danger. A danger that I believe is among us, and threatens us all.

Jonathan and Van Helsing go, separately. Mina speaks to the audience.

Mina   Although we were staying with Doctor Seward, I had to wait until he had finished his morning duties before I could speak with him. Then he told me of Lucy's death – and of what happened after it . . .

Mina falters in her speech, obviously upset by what she has learned, but she continues, attempting to overcome her distress. As she speaks, Seward enters and approaches her.

Mina   To think of her as I'd always known her – as I saw her last – of her dying like that – that was bad enough – but to think of what she had become – having to endure a second death – I was silent when he told me – I said nothing – there was nothing to be said – I could not say how I felt – I did not know what I should feel – and then – for a moment – I saw – the world that she had entered – the dark world where she had walked – for a moment, it opened up before me –

Seward speaks to Mina.

Seward   Mrs Harker –

Mina turns to him, as if coming out of a trance.

Mina   Doctor Seward – I'm sorry –

Seward   Yes, I understand . . .

Mina   You were speaking of someone –

Seward   A patient here – Renfield. I believe that he too, in some way, may be connected with this.

Mina   Tell me of him.

Seward   I can do more than that. If you wish it, if you feel able, you may see him –

Mina   I do wish it. Yes. Yes, I will.

Mina and Seward go.

SCENE 2

Renfield enters, alone, carrying his box. He looks around nervously, then squats on the floor, opens the box, and begins to eat greedily what is inside, cramming it into his mouth. When he has finished, he looks in the box, turns it upside down, shakes it, then drops it on the floor. Then he looks up, as if at some sound, or the awareness of a presence.

Renfield Is this all? No more?

Renfield stands and he speaks out, as if to some unseen presence.

No more for me? Flies. Spiders. You send them to me, yes. Drifting in on golden rays of light. A little sustenance. Your gift to me, so gracious. But not enough. They're not . . . enough! You promised more. Rats, you said, you would bring. Meat, blood. Blood is life. I waited. I still wait. I have been faithful. And this is all!

He picks up the box and holds it up.

You and I, we are of the same kind. You understand. You know my desire. There should be more, more for me, there should be more than this!

Bennett and Withers enter behind Renfield.

Bennett Renfield!

Renfield starts at his name but he does not turn round. He holds the box to his chest, hiding it, draws himself upright and composes himself, staring outwards.

You hear me, Renfield? There's a little surprise in store for you.

Withers A very nice surprise. You're going to have a visitor.

Bennett And not just any visitor, Renfield. A visitor of the female variety.

Withers A woman. A young woman.

Bennett	Friend of Doctor Seward's, or something. And she's asked to have a look round the place.
Withers	She asked to see you. God knows why she should want to, mind.
Bennett	Are you listening, Renfield? You've got a visitor. Did you hear?

*Renfield continues to keep his back to **Withers** and **Bennett** as he speaks.*

Renfield	Yes. I heard. Any friend of the good Doctor Seward is a friend of mine. She will be made more than welcome.
Withers	Going to serve her tea and cake, are you?
Renfield	Sadly, such simple, civilized amenities are not made available to me here.
Bennett	What are you doing there, Renfield? Why don't you turn round? What are you looking at out of the window?
Renfield	The evening. It's beautiful, don't you think?
Withers	It's like any other evening.
Renfield	No, it's not. Look at the colour of the sky. That deep autumn blue. This is the best time of all, I think. The turning of the year. Summer's passing, and the world rolls incessantly towards winter. And here we stand, at the cusp, held in balance between the two. Life and death co-existent. At such times, and in such light, is the heart of the world illuminated.

Renfield quotes from a poem.

Renfield	'To see a world in a grain of sand, And a Heaven in a wild flower, Hold infinity in the palm of your hand, And eternity in an hour.'
Bennett	What are you going on about, Renfield?
Renfield	Blake.

Withers	What?
Renfield	William Blake.
Bennett	Who's he when he's at home?
Withers	A mate of yours?
Renfield	A poet. I was quoting one of his poems.
Bennett	Quoting poetry, now, are you?
Renfield	I didn't expect you to have heard of him.
Withers	You expected right.
Renfield	He saw the world as it truly was. The shining world that exists beneath this world of shadows. The eternal, everlasting world. Angels and devils. Heaven and hell. From the struggle between these two, life draws its raw energy.
Bennett	You know what, Renfield? What you said just then? I didn't understand a blessed word of it!
Withers	Load of nonsense, if you ask me.
Renfield	They said Blake was mad, too.
Bennett	Mad, was he? But did he eat flies?
Withers	And spiders? Did he eat spiders, Renfield?
Bennett	I bet he didn't. That's your speciality, isn't it?
Renfield	It may have been that once I . . . entertained such a notion. That by the consumption of living creatures, one could extend one's own life. Perhaps indefinitely. But that, I know now, was a delusion. A psychosis, of which I have been cured.
Withers	Cured, are you?
Renfield	I have applied to Doctor Seward for release.
Bennett	Oh, yes, we know all about that, don't we?
Withers	We do. And I'll tell you what else we know. You ain't going to get it.

Bennett	Doctor Seward'll never release you, Renfield. And do you know why? [To **Withers**] Tell him why.
Withers	Cos you're a looney. That's why. You're stark raving mad.
Renfield	[*Quoting*] 'I am but mad north-north-west; when the wind is southerly, I know a hawk from a handsaw.' Shakespeare. Surely even you have heard of him.
Bennett	What's your game?
Renfield	Game?
Bennett	What are you up to, eh?
Renfield	I don't understand –

Withers and Bennett approach Renfield.

| Withers | Yes, you do. You're up to something. All this fancy talk, trying to pretend you're better. What is it, eh? What's going on in that nasty little head of yours? |
| Renfield | I'm sure I don't know what you mean – |

Renfield turns to them. They see the box.

Bennett	Don't you, then? Cured, are you? So what's this? [*Indicating the box*] Still up to your old tricks?
Withers	What's in it? Flies, or spiders?
Bennett	Or something bigger?

Renfield opens the box and shows it to them.

Renfield	It's empty. You see?
Withers	You won't need it any more, then, will you?
Renfield	What?
Bennett	Seeing as you're cured.
Withers	Might as well give it up.

*Withers holds his hand out for the box. **Renfield's** composure begins to crack a little, and he makes to draw the box away from*

*Withers. But **Withers** snatches it from him and puts it in his pocket. At that moment, **Seward** and **Mina** enter.*

Seward	Renfield. I'd like you to meet someone.

*Renfield turns from **Withers** and **Bennett** to **Seward** and **Mina**. He reacts to **Mina**.*

Renfield	I was told I was to have a visitor. But I didn't realize ... it would be one so ... exquisite.

*He approaches **Mina**.*

Madam. I am more than honoured to welcome you to my ... humble abode.

He bows.

Mina	Thank you, Mr Renfield.
Renfield	I only wish I could offer you more suitable hospitality. But, as you can see –
Mina	It's no matter.
Renfield	Ah, but it does, it does matter. To me. However, I have great hopes of soon being released from this place, back into the world. And then, perhaps, we may meet under more comfortable circumstances.
Mina	*[To **Seward**]* Is that so, Doctor Seward? Is Mr Renfield to be released?
Seward	He has asked me to consider the matter. And ... I am considering it.
Renfield	I hope not too long, Doctor.
Seward	We shall have to wait and see.
Renfield	I bow to your judgement, of course. *[To **Mina**]* Madam, you have the advantage of me.
Mina	In what way, Mr Renfield?
Renfield	In that you know my name, but I do not know yours.

Mina	Forgive me. I should have introduced myself. I am Mrs Harker.

Renfield starts visibly at the name.

Renfield	Harker? Mrs Harker, did you say?
Mina	Yes –
Seward	What's the matter, Renfield?

*During the following, **Renfield** begins to grow agitated.*

Renfield	Your husband is . . . Jonathan Harker?
Mina	That's right! Do you know him?
Renfield	Yes . . . no . . . I've heard of him . . . I had some business once with his employer . . . in the days when . . . before I came here . . .
Mina	Mr Hawkins – ?
Renfield	Yes . . . that's the man . . . he . . . mentioned your husband's name to me . . .
Mina	Favourably, I hope.
Renfield	What?
Mina	I said –
Renfield	[*Growing more anxious and agitated*] You're his wife, then. Mrs Harker. Mrs Jonathan Harker.
Bennett	I should watch him, Doctor Seward.
Withers	Looks like he's heading for one of his turns again.
Seward	Yes. Perhaps we should –
Renfield	And you're here! You've come here!
Mina	Mr Renfield –
Renfield	In this place! Here! Now!
Seward	[*To **Mina**] I think we ought to leave –

Renfield	*[Urgently and intensely]* Yes! Oh, yes! You ought to leave! Certainly you ought to leave!
Seward	He sometimes gets distressed like this . . . and he can become violent –
Renfield	But you won't. No. You won't leave. He won't let you.
Mina	What do you mean?
Bennett	He don't mean anything.
Withers	It's all just his ravings.
Seward	Come, Mrs Harker –
Renfield	Because you're beautiful . . . so beautiful . . . even more than she was . . . your skin so soft –

Renfield puts out a hand to touch Mina's face. She cries out and draws back. Bennett and Withers grab hold of him roughly.

Bennett	That's enough of that!
Withers	Didn't take you long, did it?
Mina	No! Don't! Don't hurt him! Poor man! He can't help himself. Can't you see how wretched he is?

Bennett and Withers let go of Renfield. He stares at Mina, in shock at her kind words.

Renfield	I am. I am . . . wretched. I am in hell.
Seward	*[To Mina]* We should go, now.
Mina	Yes. I've seen enough.

Seward and Mina go. Bennett and Withers approach Renfield again.

Bennett	Cured, then, are you?
Withers	Ready to go back into the world?
Bennett	You know what, Renfield? Somehow I don't think so.
Withers	Cos you're a nasty little piece of work. That's what you are.

Renfield	Oh, yes. Thoroughly nasty.
Bennett	And that's why you're here.
Withers	And that's why you're going to stay here. Forever.
Renfield	Not just me, though. All of us. All nasty pieces of work. You and I. No difference between us. All beasts with our snouts in the trough –

Bennett hits Renfield.

Bennett	Speak for yourself.

Withers hits Renfield.

Withers	You're the beast, not us.

Bennett hits Renfield again.

Bennett	The lowest kind of beast.

Withers hits Renfield again. Renfield falls to his knees, clutching his stomach and gasping.

Withers	So, just you remember that.

Bennett and Withers turn to go. Withers stops and turns back.

Withers	Here, Renfield. You'll need this.

*He takes the box from his pocket and drops it in front of **Renfield**. **Withers** and **Bennett** go. **Renfield** remains still for a while, attempting to recover. Then he shudders. All pretence at his being 'cured' has now gone. Almost against his will, he picks up the box, grimacing, as if it is hateful and monstrous to him. Then, in a sudden, impulsive act of rage and frustration at what he is, he crushes the box, crying out as he does so.*

Renfield	No!

He drops the crushed box on the floor and sits still. He remains onstage throughout the following scene.

SCENE 3

Mrs Outhwaite and Jonathan enter, on another part of the stage.
Mrs Outhwaite is talking to Jonathan as she enters. She speaks
with a Yorkshire accent.

Mrs Outhwaite You want to know about Carfax Manor, do you? Well, I'm the person to tell you, if there's anybody can. Though it's not a subject I'm too fond of these days.

Jonathan You're caretaker there, aren't you?

Mrs Outhwaite That's right. Been caretaker there these past ten years. Though if you want the job, you're welcome to it. I've done with the place. I'm resigning my position as from tomorrow, even though I'll feel the want of the money. For while there may be many things money will buy, I've never known it buy peace of mind. And I haven't had peace of mind there these last two months or so. Neither peace of mind nor spirit. What is it you want to know?

Jonathan I'm interested in a delivery that may have been made there recently – a delivery of . . . goods, round about the beginning of August.

Mrs Outhwaite And what might you be wanting to know about that for?

Jonathan I'm a lawyer. The whereabouts of these goods are of some legal importance.

Mrs Outhwaite I'll tell you, then. It's with the delivery of them . . . goods that all my troubles began. Goods, you call them. Boxes, I call them. Wooden boxes full of God knows what. The very day them boxes were delivered, that's the day I stopped having peace of mind and spirit.

Jonathan These boxes. Do you know where they came from?

Mrs Outhwaite Off that ship. That ship that came in with the storm. You might've known there were summat funny about them, coming off a ship that were steered by a dead man. You know about that, do you?

Jonathan	Yes ... I had heard something ...
Mrs Outhwaite	It were Alf Tranter had the delivery of them. Six of them, there were. He brought them up on his cart, and it took him and his three lads to shift each one of them into the house. Right heavy, they were. I asked him what were in them, and do you know what he said to me? 'Mould,' he said. 'They're full of mould. Like summat's gone and died in them.' And it were from the minute them boxes were put in the old place that things started turning queer.
Jonathan	In what way?
Mrs Outhwaite	Noises, for one.
Jonathan	Noises?
Mrs Outhwaite	That's right, sir. Noises. Now, I know old houses make noises, and when you've worked in a place you get to know them. They're kind of friendly, if you take my meaning. But these noises, they're summat different altogether.
Jonathan	How are they ... different?
Mrs Outhwaite	Unholy. That's how I call them. Unholy and unwholesome. Whisperings. Murmurings. Scratchings. Like something with claws scratching and scraping its way along the floors. First time I heard it, I were in there giving the place a bit of an airing, and I were standing just by the cellar door, and up it comes from down below. That scratching and scraping. Sent me cold, it did. And that weren't the last time I heard it, either. And always from the same place.
Jonathan	The cellar?
Mrs Outhwaite	That's right. The cellar. Where me and Alf Tranter put them boxes. But it weren't just noises. It takes more than a few unwholesome noises to put the wind up a woman like me.
Jonathan	What else?
Mrs Outhwaite	Rats, sir. The place is full of them. There's always been a few rats there, of course. Can't help it, an old place like that, and

it's been empty for nigh on a century. But it's more than just a few I'm talking about. There's a whole multitude of them. And big, bigger than any natural rat has a right to be. I came upon one of them just a week or so back, perched atop of the stairs, and looking down at me. Well, I weren't going to be outfaced by no rat, so I went up them stairs waving my broom at it, but the blessed thing just stood there staring at me with them red eyes and big yellow teeth. And I'm not ashamed to say I backed off from it, sir. But I'll tell you this about it. I had a good look at it when I were on the stairs, and there were blood on its mouth. Fresh blood. And where that blood came from don't bear the thinking about.

Jonathan   Have you ever seen any human figure about the house?

Mrs Outhwaite   I can't say that I have, no. I've not seen nobody. Though sometimes I've had a kind of sense of somebody being there. Like I were being watched. But the only thing I've ever seen is them rats. And another creature.

Jonathan   What kind of creature?

Mrs Outhwaite   Well, now, when that ship come in out of the storm, it were all in the newspaper as how there were summat else on board, apart from the dead man. A dog, they said it were. A big dog that came jumping out the hold and ran off into the town.

They said nobody saw it again after that, nor knew what had become of it. But somebody did. Somebody saw it. I did. And it weren't no dog.

Jonathan	What was it?

Mrs Outhwaite   I only caught sight of it the once. In the wood that grows at the back of the house. It were getting dark, but I saw it there, coming out of the trees. It stopped when it saw me, and looked me full in the face before it turned round and went back into the wood. I've only seen summat like it once before, years ago, when I were a young woman and went down to London and paid a visit to the zoo. But I'll swear on any Bible you like that this creature were the same as I'd seen there. It were a wolf.

Jonathan   A wolf?

Mrs Outhwaite   I don't care if you don't believe me –

Jonathan   I do believe you, Mrs Outhwaite. And you have been most helpful. Thank you. Please, take this for your trouble.

He gives her some money.

Mrs Outhwaite   I won't refuse you. I'll be in need of a bit of brass now I've decided to quit that place. It'll be in short supply. But I'll have something I don't have now. Peace of mind, sir. Peace of mind and spirit.

Mrs Outhwaite and Jonathan go, separately.

• •

SCENE 4

Renfield looks up and stands, suddenly, aware and alert. He speaks aloud to himself, with a mixture of fear and anticipation.

Renfield   Night comes. The dark. And with it . . . the thing of the dark. Shadows fall, a mist gathers, creeps along the ground. See! He comes! And all hell's creatures with him.

Renfield quotes from 'Hamlet'. As he speaks, Dracula enters behind him.

Renfield	'Tis now the very witching time of night, When churchyards yawn, and hell itself breathes out Contagion to this world. Now could I drink hot blood – '

*Renfield breaks off, aware of **Dracula's** presence.*

Renfield	No more. Words fail me. He's here.
Dracula	Yes. I am here.
Renfield	Master.
Dracula	Won't you turn and look at me?
Renfield	Yes, Master.

*Renfield turns to face **Dracula**.*

Dracula	There is fear in your eyes.
Renfield	Of course –

*Dracula approaches **Renfield**.*

Dracula	And something else. Something other than fear –
Renfield	Master! She was here. I have seen her!
Dracula	Yes. I know. I feel her presence. Her warmth. Her scent fills the air. You spoke with her?
Renfield	Yes!
Dracula	I too shall speak with her soon. She will hear my voice. And then she will hear no other.
Renfield	She will be yours.
Dracula	Mine, yes. And no one this time shall take her back.
Renfield	And for me?
Dracula	For you?
Renfield	What for me?
Dracula	Do you not like what I send you?
Renfield	Spiders, flies, birds –

Dracula	It is life.
Renfield	But not enough. Small, mean lives –
Dracula	So is your life small and mean. This is what you are.
Renfield	I am of your kind –
Dracula	No! You are not of my kind! You shall never be! You are – as you are. Be content with it.
Renfield	No!

*Suddenly, **Dracula** grabs **Renfield** by the throat.*

Dracula	No? You would say no to me! You would dare! You know how I could crush you, little man. Crush you out of all existence, like one of those insects you feed upon. It would mean nothing to me. You live because I choose you to live. And if I choose you to die – you die.

*He squeezes **Renfield's** throat, choking him. Then, he throws him down to the floor. **Renfield** gasps.*

Dracula	There. I choose you to live – for now. And I give you something. Your freedom.
Renfield	Freedom?
Dracula	To leave this place. Your attendants sleep. The door to your cell is open. Your path is clear. Go.

***Renfield** now realizes that **Dracula** has abandoned him. He speaks in despair.*

Renfield	Go? Go where? Where would I go? What is there for me out there?
Dracula	The same as here. Nothing. I have done with you, Renfield. For a while you . . . amused me. Now I put you from me. But for the small services you have done, I make you this gift. Your life.
Renfield	It is no life!
Dracula	Then die. That too may be a gift.

Dracula approaches Renfield.

Renfield   No – no –

Renfield scurries off stage in fear. Dracula turns from him and speaks aloud to himself.

Dracula   She sleeps here tonight. For safety, she thinks. I hear her breathing, soft. I hear the delicate rustle of her skin, her hair. I hear the whispering of her most secret dreams, dreams she hardly even hears herself. But she will know them. For they call to me.

Dracula goes.

• •

SCENE 5

Van Helsing enters and speaks to the audience.

Van Helsing   This is what I have learned of Count Dracula. These are the few facts I have gathered, and this is what I told the others when I returned. He has been known in the East for many centuries. First, as a warrior of noble race, who fought for his homeland against the Turk. A man of courage, great intelligence, strength, and iron will. And merciless in his dealings with the enemy. Merciless and cruel. And a man of whom it was whispered, even then, that he had dealings with the Evil One. A pact was made, perhaps. His soul for the immortality of life. Or simply the will was so strong that even death could not subdue it. Whatever the cause, he passed from natural life to life unnatural, from being mortal man to Nosferatu. The undead. Wampyr. Vampire. So he has lived on, through the centuries, feeding upon the blood of the living, making of them others of his kind. But all these are lesser beings than he. For though he has long ago shed the last of his humanity, though he has become monster, yet that will, that intellect, that merciless intelligence lives on, and, like him, they have grown strong in power. Strong and terrible. And he reigns alone, supreme.

Seward, Holmwood, Morris, Jonathan, and Mina enter on their lines and speak to the audience. Mina wears a lace shawl.

Seward	This is the enemy that has come among us.
Holmwood	This is the corruption that dwells in our midst.
Morris	The darkness that has taken root in our hearts.
Jonathan	The darkness that must be destroyed.
Mina	For if not it will surely grow, and spread until it has consumed us all.

Van Helsing turns and speaks to them.

Van Helsing	Yes, indeed. And this is why we are met here together. To see what means are at our disposal for our battle against the foe. For the danger is imminent, and we must act with all urgency.
Seward	Even more urgency now that Renfield has escaped.
Jonathan	He's still at large?
Morris	Arthur and I have been helping to search for him all day. It's as if he's just vanished from the face of the earth.
Van Helsing	No. He will be near, but hidden. He is slave to Dracula. He will not be able to go far from his master. But he is of little account to us at the moment. It is on the master that we must fix our attention.
Holmwood	I think there's one thing that should be done first.
Van Helsing	What's that?
Holmwood	From what Jonathan has told us, Mina is the most immediately vulnerable. Isn't that so?
Jonathan	Yes.
Holmwood	Then it would be best to remove her from that danger. She should leave now, and return to London.
Van Helsing	Well, Mrs Harker? What do you say to that?
Mina	I appreciate your concern for my welfare, Arthur. But I am

determined to play my part in destroying this monster. I shall not go. I shall stay.

Holmwood [*To Mina*] I saw what happened to Lucy. If the same were to happen to you –

Mina I'm quite resolved. I shall not be ... packed off to London. I shall remain here, where I may do some good.

Van Helsing Bravely spoken, Mrs Harker. Your courage and determination shall be an example to us all. And we shall all need those qualities if we are to have any hope of succeeding in our plan.

Morris Do we have a plan?

Van Helsing What we have learned about the nature of the beast shall help us to form one. We know, for example, that the vampire rises only at night. During the day he must rest. And he must rest in his native earth. That is the reason the boxes were brought here. They are his sanctuary from the sun, which is deadly to him.

Jonathan And we know where those boxes are. And if we can prevent him from returning to them –

Seward [*Interrupting*] Wouldn't it be simpler to deal with him as we dealt with – ?

Holmwood You can say it, John. As we dealt with Lucy. Yes, those are my thoughts exactly.

Van Helsing We may yet have to. But not now. It is too late. In a short time the sun will be setting. We could not reach Carfax Manor in time to take him at his rest. He will be rising soon, going about his business. But, while he is away, we shall strike our first blow. Contaminate the earth in the boxes, so that he cannot return to his lair.

Morris Drive him into the open, where we can face him outright?

Van Helsing Exactly so, Mr Morris.

Seward And then?

Van Helsing	Then, weakened by the sun's rays, we shall have him at our mercy – and, with weapons of goodness, and trust in God, we shall drive him at last from earth into hell where he belongs.
Holmwood	I wish I thought it would be as simple as it sounds.
Van Helsing	You're right to speak words of caution, Mr Holmwood. We must not underestimate his cunning and his intelligence. But I have reason to believe he has urgent business to hand. And his urgency may cause him to be careless – and in that may lie our advantage, and our victory.
Morris	The sun's going down.
Van Helsing	Then we must be about our business. Mrs Harker, you will stay here? I think it best you do.
Mina	Yes.
Van Helsing	And Mr Harker, you will remain with your wife. Safeguard the room from entry, as I've shown you.
Jonathan	I will.
Van Helsing	Go. Do it now.

Jonathan goes.

Doctor Seward, Mr Holmwood, Mr Morris – make yourselves ready for this night's business. Our weapons are downstairs. I wish to speak with Mrs Harker privately a moment. I'll join you shortly.

Seward, Holmwood, and Morris go. Van Helsing turns to Mina.

Van Helsing	He will come for you again tonight.
Mina	Again? You know?
Van Helsing	Yes. You wear a shawl about your neck. To hide the marks. And there are other signs that I have learned. It was last night?
Mina	Last night, yes.
Van Helsing	Does your husband know?

Mina	No. I hardly knew myself – I thought it was a bad dream – until I looked in the mirror.
Van Helsing	Are you strong enough to resist him?
Mina	I shall try to be.
Van Helsing	I know you shall. There is a quality within you that is rare. A strength, a courage of the soul. It is that which draws him to you. And it is that which will help to defeat him.
Mina	I pray to God it will.
Van Helsing	Just this one night, Mrs Harker. One night, and, with the dawn that follows, you shall be rid of him.

Van Helsing turns and goes.
Mina remains onstage.

SCENE 6

Mina speaks to the audience. As she does so, she draws back the curtain to reveal the French window.

Mina	The sun set. Night came. I went to our room. Flowers of garlic were hung from the window frames. A crucifix stood, bravely, on the table. A smaller crucifix, on a chain, hung at my neck. But I knew they would all be to no avail. Already Jonathan lay, in a heavy sleep, across the bed. Already a mist was gathering outside. Already the room was filled with a sweet, heavy scent. And, as if from somewhere far off, or as if from somewhere deep inside, his voice spoke.

Dracula enters at the far side of the stage.

Dracula	What are these trinkets against my power? This primitive magic has no authority over me.

Mina continues to speak to the audience.

Mina	I took down the flowers of garlic from the window frame. I loosened the catch, pushed the glass wide. The night air touched my face, a soft sigh of content. But there was nothing beyond, nothing to be seen. Only thick mist, congealing to some outward form. I turned back to the room. I crossed to the bed and kissed Jonathan as he lay sleeping. I brushed the hair from his eyes. Then all collapsed, and was made new again, and I turned back, and he was there.

Dracula approaches Mina. He stops and speaks to her.

Dracula	Remove that.
Mina	[To the audience] He pointed to the crucifix at my neck. I took it off and dropped it to the floor.
Dracula	Come here to me.
Mina	[To the audience] I went across to him. I stood before him. His shadow was upon me, and my soul shivered.

Mina approaches Dracula.

Dracula	You are afraid.
Mina	Yes.
Dracula	There is no need to be. No need to fear me.
Mina	No need?
Dracula	You think I bring you death, but I bring you life.
Mina	I know what you bring. If it were death, I would welcome it. But it is neither life nor death. Something unholy, abominable –
Dracula	[Interrupting] You know nothing of which you speak! Nothing! How could you know? My existence is ... unimaginable to any of mortal flesh. The world you walk in, the world of light and

sun that is your only reality, is to me a thing of mist and rags and shadows. It is frail as a spider's web compared to mine. For mine is a world eternal and unchanging, a world of bottomless depths and endless horizons. It is a world where silence has a voice, and sings the frozen void between the stars. This is my world. And it shall be yours.

Mina   Mine? What do you mean?

Dracula   For centuries I have walked my world alone. In fierce joy, but in weariness too. The weariness of solitude. For so long I have yearned for a companion to share with me this world, this eternity. So I shall walk alone no more. One shall walk beside me. You. You shall be my companion.

Mina   No –

Dracula   Listen! I could feed on you as I have fed on others. You would become undead, feed on others in your turn. Yet I sense in you a kinship, a likeness to myself. The same proud spirit, the same strong will. Is it not so? Do you not sense something of it yourself?

Mina says nothing.

Dracula   You do not deny it. You know. It is our destiny to walk together, to feed upon this world, devour it all. And so, I do not force you. I do not feed upon you. But ask you to come to me willingly. To become as I, equal and free. To feed upon me.

He holds out his hand to her.

Dracula   Come.

Mina takes a step towards him, then pulls back.

Mina   I will not! No!

Dracula snarls in rage.

Dracula   You shall not deny me! You shall be mine!

Mina   Perhaps. But never willingly.

Dracula	Then your husband is dead. Even as he lies there sleeping, I shall crush him, tear his throat, feed on him before your eyes –
Mina	No!
Dracula	Then come to me. Come to me and he lives. Though I hate him, I shall let him live, for you. Will you do this for him? Will you give him his life?

Mina pauses for a moment.

Mina	Yes. For love of him. For you I have nothing but hate.
Dracula	That will not be for long. Soon, he will be nothing to you. And I – we – shall be all.

He steps back from her.

Dracula	Come. Let us make our pact.

*Mina turns and speaks to the audience. As she speaks, **Dracula** goes.*

Mina	What that pact was, and how it was made, I have not told anyone, nor will ever tell. But there, in the dark of the room, it seemed my soul floated from my body, and crossed immense spaces, and I saw great forests and dark mountains, and a wide plain stretching between them. And all was sharp and clear and bright. And where the earth ended, the mountains rose, and there was yet more beyond the mountains, and I was running, and the horizons rolled beneath my feet, and there was no end to them.

Mina turns and goes.

● ●

SCENE 7

Jonathan enters and speaks to the audience.

Jonathan	They woke me in the early hours of the morning. Mina was still sleeping, and they called me out of the room, not to disturb her. There were only the two of them, and I could tell by their faces that something was terribly wrong.

Van Helsing and Seward enter and approach Jonathan. They are distressed, and in a state of fear and alarm.

Van Helsing	Wrong, yes! All wrong! We should have known he could not be taken so easily.
Jonathan	What do you mean? Where are the others?
Seward	Dead.
Jonathan	No –
Van Helsing	I'm sorry, yes.
Jonathan	Tell me what happened.
Seward	We came to the Manor some time after sunset. All was dark and silent. Arthur and Quincey remained by the door, to keep watch. The Professor and I went inside, down to the cellar. We found the boxes. But there were only four.
Jonathan	Four? But –
Van Helsing	Two must have been removed to some other place for safety. It was then we realized that Dracula must have guessed our plans. Nonetheless, we set about our work. Removed the lids from the remaining boxes. Sprinkled holy water on the earth, placed crosses there, so that they were no longer refuge for the undead.
Seward	But then, just as we were finishing, we heard cries from above. We raced back up the stairs and outside, and there we saw … four … creatures … I still don't know what they were – wolf or human. It's impossible to say.
Van Helsing	They were creatures of hell, come at Dracula's bidding. And they had struck down those poor men, and were feeding upon them.
Jonathan	My God –
Seward	I heard them feeding, heard the sound of their jaws tearing and ripping. And then … then they looked up – and I saw their faces –

ACT 3　SCENE 7

97

| Van Helsing | They would have leapt on us too, torn out our throats. But the crucifix checked them. Armed with the holy weapon, we advanced, and they fell back snarling, turned at last, and disappeared into the darkness of the wood. |

| Jonathan | And Arthur, and Quincey – ? |

| Seward | There was nothing we could do for them. Arthur was already dead. Quincey died as we knelt beside him. |

| Jonathan | Where are they now? |

| Van Helsing | We took their bodies into the house. I laid the crucifix upon them to protect them from further desecration. Tomorrow we must return, and give them a proper burial. |

| Jonathan | Yes ... of course ... but what's to be done now? |

| Van Helsing | I confess, I'm not certain ... we have failed. He foresaw all, and led us into his trap. And he is still at large. We must ... think again. For this is a foe indeed to be feared. |

Jonathan, Seward, and Van Helsing go.

• •

SCENE 8

Mina enters and speaks to the audience.

| Mina | So I knew at last that it must be me. When I learned from Professor Van Helsing and Doctor Seward what had happened, when I saw their weakened, exhausted faces, when I saw how the shock of it struck at Jonathan, brought back to him the horror of his own experiences – then I knew that I, and I alone, must destroy this monster. For what the monster was, I too was now, in part. And the strength he had given me could be turned against him. |

Mina pauses before continuing. As she speaks Renfield enters, behind her.

| Mina | So I went back to where it had all begun. To the churchyard by the abbey, on the clifftop above the sea. And I thought of how Lucy and I had walked there, in the summer, how she'd |

told me of her engagement, how we'd talked and laughed together and planned our futures, and how full of life and love and hope we had both been. And I thought too of Mr Swales, and the storm, and the ship, and of the darkness that had come with the storm and the ship. And it seemed as I thought of those things, that as all had begun there, all the evil and horror, so there too it must end.

Cautiously, **Renfield** *approaches* **Mina.**

Renfield	You've come to seek him?

Mina starts and turns to **Renfield.**

Mina	Yes.
Renfield	But you find only me.
Mina	Where you are, he will not be far.
Renfield	It's true – yes – he binds me to him – holds me fast – my soul in his fist – squeezing – 'You are free,' he said – but he knows I can never be free – not until –
Mina	He is destroyed.
Renfield	[With sudden passion] Yes! Destroyed! You will destroy him?
Mina	If I can.
Renfield	But you are – you are like him –
Mina	No –
Renfield	Of his kind –
Mina	No –
Renfield	Yes! He has taken you to him. He is making you as he is. It works in you – the power – growing – the dark in your heart – the hunger –
Mina	Not yet! I fight it. I will destroy him, and destroy the darkness within me.
Renfield	Not alone. Too much of you belongs to him. At the end you would falter. But together, you and I –

99

Mina	*[Taken aback]* You?
Renfield	*[Determined]* Yes! I will be free of him at last. He burns in me, he scalds my soul! I wish to be – a man again.
Mina	You know where he is?
Renfield	There. In the abbey. The crypt. He lies there now. You go to him, walk with him in the dark. Keep him with you all night. I shall defile his earth, give him no sanctuary. Then, when the day comes, he will die. Go now. The sun is setting. He will rise soon, and you must be there to greet him.

Renfield goes. **Mina** *speaks to the audience.*

| Mina | As the sky reddened I went to the abbey. As the last rays of light splashed upon its walls, I walked among its ruined stones, entered the broken doorway, descended to the dark beneath the earth. And there I found him. |

Dracula *enters and speaks to* **Mina.**

| Dracula | I knew you would come. |

Mina *continues to tell her story to the audience.*

| Mina | Together in the dark we stood, and I could feel part of me drawing towards him, longing to embrace the world of his making, the monstrous, the merciless, the unfettered. And that |

part I let go to him – but kept another secret, held precious and safe.

Dracula *[To Mina]* Tonight I shall not feed. It is not yet necessary. We shall make our pact again. You shall draw blood from me once more, come closer to the eternal life.

Mina *[Turning to speak to Dracula]* Yes. But not here. Outside, on the clifftop.

Dracula The place you first saw me, when I fed on the other?

Mina Yes, there.

Dracula It's fitting. Where it began, it shall end. And a new life begin.

Mina turns back to speak to the audience.

Mina Such visions I saw that night. Wonders and terrors. I saw the ages of the world, saw how life in those ages flowered and withered, brief as a breath, an insect thing. And there, apart from it all, drawing life from the living, one creature unchanging. Myself. And I stood among the ruins of creation, and the earth was waste about me, and my soul cried out, and there was nothing to hear.

Dracula *[To Mina]* It is almost finished now. You feel the power growing in you. Soon there will be nothing but that power. You will shed your mortality like a dry skin. And then you will know the rapture and the glory, the terrible joy, the insatiable hunger.

Mina *[To the audience]* In the east, the sky was lightening. The morning wind blew in fresh from the sea. On the earth, the dew glimmered. In the sky, the stars dimmed.

Dracula *[To Mina]* I must go now. Seek me out again tomorrow night. Then our pact shall be sealed, and together we shall hunt, and feed.

Renfield enters. He screams at Dracula in hatred.

Renfield No! You will never hunt or feed again!

*Dracula wheels round to **Renfield**. **Mina** steps aside and watches the following scene with growing horror.*

Renfield	Never stalk the night earth, never prey upon the living. Never, never again! Not even flies and spiders, Master! See the light! See the sun! The master must go, he must seek his hiding place. Hide from the sun. But where? Where can he hide? Nowhere!
Dracula	What do you mean? What have you done?
Renfield	No sanctuary, no place of rest! All are closed to him now. Holy water, God's flesh. They drive him out, drive him to his death!
Dracula	You have betrayed me!
Renfield	Yes, Master. Poor Renfield! Wretched Renfield. Renfield who was nothing to you. You had done with me! Now I have done with you! She and I together. The one you cast aside, and the one you chose. We destroy you. The spider caught in his own web. Soon you'll be no more. All will be free, all that have been taken, free of you. I shall be free. I shall be a man again!

*Swiftly and savagely, **Dracula** grabs **Renfield** by the throat. **Mina** cries out.*

Mina	No!

*Mina runs to help **Renfield** but **Dracula** knocks her down. He squeezes **Renfield** by the throat. **Renfield** gasps, struggles, then falls silent and still. His body hangs heavy. **Dracula** lets him drop to the floor.*

Dracula	My last act in this world.

He turns and speaks to the audience.

Now let day come. Let the sun rise. Let the light of your world burn me to dust. It shall know me no more, and I leave it with my undying hate!

*Dracula freezes. **Mina** rises, speaking to the audience as she does so.*

Mina	Then the sky burst into flame, and he gave a cry, a long howl of anguish and pain and rage and despair. And as it rose, the light seared through him, and he was gone, leaving nothing but dust that was taken by the wind and scattered across the face of the deep.
	Blackout. In the blackout, there is a loud, terrifying cry, rising, echoing, then dying to silence.

● ●

SCENE 9

*The lights come up on an empty stage. **Van Helsing, Seward, and Jonathan** enter on their lines, and stand one at either side, and one at the back of the stage. They speak to the audience.*

Van Helsing	So we had come through the flames and were purged of evil. Though it had cost us dear, the enemy had been defeated and good, as it always must, prevailed.
Seward	But the wounds of the battle had gone deep, and though some at last healed, we bore the scars always. All had lost something. None would ever be the same.
Jonathan	So we went back to what we could salvage of our lives. We settled, had children, lived comfortably, though not in great prosperity. And if ever we spoke of that desperate time, it was as of something long past and done with, for, in the end, we had peace of spirit and mind.
	Mina enters and stands centre stage. She speaks to the audience.
Mina	But still even now I dream. And in my dream I'm standing beneath a great expanse of sky, lit by numberless stars, and ahead of me is a wide grassland, stretching out into the distance where the black shadows of mountains rise. And all is clear and sharp and bright, and there's such silence, such longing, and the moon is full and we are wolves and we are running, and the horizons roll endlessly beneath our feet.

THE END

Activities

Year 7

Key Stage 3 Framework Objectives		Relevant Activities Chapter(s)
Sentence Level		
1	Subordinate clauses	Introducing Dracula, Literary Heritage
11	Sentence variety	Literary Heritage
18	Sentences in older text	Introducing Dracula, Literary Heritage
Word Level		
15	Dictionary and thesaurus	Introducing Dracula, Literary Heritage
22	Words in different languages	Introducing Dracula
Reading		
1	Locate information	Introducing Dracula, Story Structure
2	Extract information	Narrative Techniques, Literary Heritage
4	Note-making	Introducing Dracula, Story Structure, Literary Heritage
7	Identify main ideas	Introducing Dracula, Story Structure
8	Infer and deduce	Introducing Dracula
9	Distinguish writer's views	Introducing Dracula, Narrative Techniques
12	Character, setting and mood	Introducing Dracula
14	Language choices	Introducing Dracula
15	Endings	Story Structure
20	Literary heritage	Literary Heritage
Writing		
1	Drafting process	Introducing Dracula, Narrative Techniques
2	Planning formats	Story Structure, Narrative Techniques
6	Characterisation	Introducing Dracula
8	Visual and sound effects	Introducing Dracula
9	Link writing and reading	Introducing Dracula
10	Organise texts appropriately	Narrative Techniques
12	Develop logic	Narrative Techniques
14	Evocative description	Narrative Techniques
15	Express a view	Narrative Techniques
16	Validate an argument	Narrative Techniques
Speaking and Listening		
12	Exploratory talk	A New Scene
13	Collaboration	A New Scene
Drama		
15	Explore in role	Narrative Techniques
16	Collaborate on scripts	A New Scene
17	Extend spoken repertoire	A New Scene
19	Evaluate presentations	A New Scene

Year 8

Key Stage 3 Framework Objectives	Relevant Activities Chapter(s)
Sentence Level	
2 Variety of sentence structure	Literary Heritage
8 Subject-specific conventions	Narrative Techniques
9 Adapting text types	Narrative Techniques
13 Change over time	Introducing Dracula, Literary Heritage
14 Compare languages	Introducing Dracula
Word Level	
9 Specialist vocabulary	Introducing Dracula, Literary Heritage
14 Language change	Introducing Dracula
Reading	
1 Combine information	Literary Heritage
2 Independent research	Literary Heritage
3 Notemaking formats	Narrative Techniques
5 Trace developments	Introducing Dracula
8 Transposition	Literary Heritage
10 Development of key ideas	Story Structure, Narrative Techniques
11 Compare treatments of same theme	Literary Heritage
14 Literary conventions	Narrative Techniques, Literary Heritage
15 Historical context	Literary Heritage
16 Cultural context	Literary Heritage
Writing	
1 Effective planning	Introducing Dracula, Narrative Techniques
2 Anticipate reader reaction	Introducing Dracula, Narrative Techniques
5 Narrative commentary	Introducing Dracula
10 Effective information	Narrative Techniques
13 Present a case persuasively	Narrative Techniques
14 Develop an argument	Narrative Techniques
Speaking and Listening	
9 Evaluate own contributions	A New Scene
11 Building on others	A New Scene
12 Varied roles in discussion	A New Scene
Drama	
13 Evaluate own drama skills	A New Scene
15 Work in role	Narrative Techniques, A New Scene
16 Collaborative presentation	A New Scene

Introducing Dracula

1   Look up the word 'prologue' in a good dictionary. Find out what it means, and investigate the origin of the word. How can the word be divided into parts? What does each part mean in the original language?

2   Now re-read the Prologue (page 12) and think about its function.

- What information does it give the reader about Dracula? How does he feel and what is he hoping for?
- How does it whet the audience's appetite for the main story?
- What atmosphere and mood does it create? (Look in particular at the final image.)

3   David Calcutt, the author of this playscript, uses the Prologue to introduce the setting, plot, and main character of the play. In pairs or small groups, consider the following.

- Are you surprised by anything that Dracula says in the Prologue?
- There are lots of films and stories about Dracula, but few portray him as lonely and weary. Why do you think David Calcutt makes Dracula express these feelings at the very start of the play?
- Does this affect the way the audience feels about Dracula?

4   In the original novel by Bram Stoker, the reader first 'meets' Dracula through Jonathan Harker, the young lawyer who travels to Transylvania to do business with the Count.

Read the following extract from the novel in which Harker describes Dracula:

His face was a strong – a very strong – aquiline, with high bridge of the thin nose and peculiarly arched nostrils; with lofty domed forehead, and hair growing scantily round the temples, but profusely elsewhere. His eyebrows were very massive, almost meeting over the nose, and with bushy hair that seemed to curl in its own profusion. The mouth, so far as I could see it under the heavy moustache, was fixed and rather cruel-looking, with peculiarly sharp white teeth; these protruded over the lips, whose remarkable ruddiness showed astonishing vitality in a man of his years. For the rest, his ears were pale and at the tops extremely pointed; the chin was broad and strong, and the cheeks firm though thin. The general effect was one of extraordinary pallor.

Hitherto I had noticed the backs of his hands as they lay on his knees in the firelight, and they had seemed rather white and fine; but seeing them now close to me, I could not but notice that they were rather coarse – broad, with squat fingers. Strange to say, there were hairs in the centre of the palm. The nails were long and fine, and cut to a sharp point. As the Count leaned over me and his hands touched me, I could not repress a shudder. It may have been that his breath was rank, but a horrible feeling of nausea came over me, which, do what I would, I could not conceal. The Count, evidently noticing it, drew back; and with a grim sort of smile, which showed more than he had yet done his protuberant teeth, sat himself down again on his own side of the fireplace. We were both silent for a while; and as I looked towards the window I saw the first dim streak of the coming dawn. There seemed a strange stillness over everything; but as I listened I heard, as if from down below in the valley, the howling of many wolves. The Count's eyes gleamed ...

5   What impression of Count Dracula do you get from this description? Consider:

- whether Harker is attracted to or repelled by Dracula
- what is odd about Dracula's appearance
- the clues that he might be a vampire
- anything attractive about Dracula's appearance
- the personal qualities suggested by this description (particularly by that of the mouth)
- the image, at the end of this extract, echoed in the Prologue of the playscript.

6   How can you tell that this is not a modern piece of writing?

- Are there words that we no longer use?
- Are there expressions that we no longer use at all, or use slightly differently today?
- Are the sentences generally long or short, simple or complex?
- What sort of punctuation is used most frequently?

7   Now it's your turn to introduce a character (not the Count) from the story. Choose a character, then write either a) a Prologue for your character to speak, or b) a narrative description of the character. Follow the steps outlined below.

> Remember: If your character is speaking the Prologue, use the first person. If your character is being described by a narrator, use the third person.

Step 1
First, select your character (choose one that you feel plays a large part in the story).

Step 2
Skim the playscript to gather details about your character – about his/her looks, personality, and behaviour towards other characters. You may need to imagine some details.

Step 3
Make notes about your character, listing all the features that you want to highlight.

Step 4
Experiment with words and phrases to find powerful, unusual descriptions.

Step 5
Use imagery to enhance the description and make it interesting for the reader (e.g. similes and metaphors).

Step 6
Attraction or repulsion? Decide how you want your audience to feel about your character from your introduction. (You could aim for mixed reactions.)

Step 7
Write a first draft and give it to a partner for their comments and suggestions.

Step 8
Revise your draft, proof-reading for spellings and punctuation.

Step 9
Display or present your character introduction.

Story Structure

1   The structure of most good stories can be divided into stages:

- opening
- plot development
- crisis
- resolution.

Each stage has different features, although the stages are linked together through the characters and the unfolding story.

Read the following summaries of the main features of each phase:

Opening

- Key people are introduced.
- A task or challenge is set.
- The setting and mood is created.
- The reader's curiosity is aroused, to make them want to read on.

Plot development

- We learn more about the characters.
- Events move swiftly to sustain the reader's interest.
- The tension is built up through more atmosphere and challenge.
- Some of the initial questions are answered, but others are asked.
- Some unexpected things happen, so the plot twists.
- More problems arise.
- (There can be mini-crises within this section, where tension is increased, then falls again.)

Crisis

- Tension mounts, as the final confrontation/challenge looms.
- At the height of the drama there is conflict, which can be verbal, physical, or mental.
- Danger, violence, and extreme emotion often feature.

Resolution/ending

- The problem is solved/the challenge is complete.
- Some characters may die or disappear, others go on with their lives.
- The reader is left with a feeling of completion, even if the resolution is unexpected.
- Sometimes, the ending links back to the beginning, or to the title of the story.

2   Skim through the playscript of *Dracula*. Trace the unfolding structure of the story, identifying some of the key features in the appropriate stages. Make notes or draw up a chart like the one started for you below.

The Structure of Dracula

Opening

- From the beginning of the Prologue to Mr Hawkins' speech in Act One, Scene One: 'It's a great opportunity for you, my boy. A great opportunity. Yes. And a great adventure!' (page 15).

- Dracula introduces himself in the Prologue

- Jonathan Harker and Mr Hawkins are introduced (as are Lucy and Mina, indirectly)

- Harker is set an important task – to take all the business documents and details to Count Dracula …

Note that the ending of one phase and the beginning of the next may not always be clear. Different views are valid if they can be justified.

3   On a graph, record how the levels of tension rise and fall during the story. Plot your graph on a simple grid like the one below. It is up to you how much detail you include in labelling the sections on the *x* axis.

high tension

medium tension

low tension

opening   *plot development*   *crisis*   *resolution*

Narrative Techniques

In the novel, the *Dracula* story is not told simply by one narrator, but through a variety of narratives, some of which are written by the main characters in the story. For example:

- letters between Mina and Lucy
- Jonathan's journal
- Dr Seward's diary
- a newspaper cutting
- a medical report
- telegrams
- business letters.

The technique of telling a story from more than one viewpoint is a common feature of late nineteenth-century novels.

What do you think are the advantages of using a variety of narrative techniques? Think about:

- the variety of viewpoints
- the mix of styles of writing
- how different accounts of the same events make unlikely events seem more credible.

NEWSPAPER REPORT

In the playscript, the story unfolds through the characters who enact actual events and describe events from the past. A dramatist cannot include all the details that novelist can, but here is an opportunity for you to fill in those details.

A heading to attract attention

A sub-heading to give a brief summary of the topic

Third person narrative (except in quotations)

Newspaper Reports

A 'gripping' first sentence to draw the reader into the article

A visual and a suitable caption

Quotations from witnesses

Why? When? Where? Who? What?

Factual information as well as opinions

1   Write and layout a full newspaper report on the storm at Whitby and the arrival of the Demeter in the harbour. Re-read Act 1, Scene 1 and decide how much of this information to include in your report. Use the spider diagram below to remind you of some key features of newspaper reports. You may wish to add other features as well.

2   Write a first draft of your newspaper report and show it to a partner. Ask for their comments and suggestions. Ask them:

●   Does it give enough information?
●   Do the paragraphs work in sequence?
●   Does the heading sound interesting?
●   How can I improve this report?

3   Revise your report, taking care to check your spellings and punctuation, before producing the final version.

A PERSUASIVE LETTER

In Bram Stoker's novel, the men decide to try to confront Dracula alone – they want to protect Mina from upset and danger. Her husband, Jonathan, writes in his diary:

> 'I am truly thankful that she is to be left out of our future work, and even of our deliberations. It is too great a strain for a woman to bear.'

Imagine you are Mina and that you are determined to join the battle against Dracula. Write a persuasive letter, giving reasons why you want to be part of the team.

Step 1
First list your reasons for wanting to join the cause. Your list might begin like this:

> Lucy was my best friend and I want to end her suffering.
>
> Dracula seems attracted to me, so maybe I can use this to advantage.
>
> I know all that has happened so far ...

As you draft your letter, think about some of the key features of persuasive texts.

- They express a personal view.
- They use repetition and rhetorical questions for effect.

- They anticipate opposing views and argue against them.
- They appeal to the reader's sense of reason and justice, as well as their emotions.

Think carefully about who you will address your letter to: your husband, Dr Seward, or Professor Van Helsing (or maybe all three?).

Step 2
Write a first draft then show it to a partner for their comments. Ask them:

- Are the reasons convincing?
- Should I include more facts?
- Does the letter appeal to your emotions as well as your common sense?
- How can I make this letter more persuasive?

Step 3
Write a final draft of your letter, taking care with punctuation and spelling.

Step 4
You could use your work for a role-play activity, in which Mina is put in the 'hot seat' and answers questions from the rest of the class or group. Think about how you envisage Mina: what her body language might convey about her personality and whether her manner and behaviour are conventional for the Victorian age.

A New Scene

1   Re-read Act 3, Scene 7, in which Van Helsing and Seward give an account of the terrible events that lead to the deaths of Arthur and Quincey.

2   In small groups, discuss, plan, write, and then act out these events. During this task, make sure that everyone gives their ideas and listens carefully to the others. At the end of the task, think about how effectively you worked with the group.

Step 1

Go through the extract carefully and sketch out the sequence of events. It might help to divide the events up into scenes (see below).

Jonathan, Seward, Van Helsing and Quincey arrive outside the Manor. They decide to split up.

Van Helsing and Jonathan are in the cellar ...

...

Step 2

Decide who will play each part. Don't forget that you need people to play the roles of the 'creatures of hell' as well as the main characters.

Step 3

Each person should think carefully about how his or her character might feel during the course of events, e.g. Quincey might feel confident and brave to begin with, then alarmed at the approach of unknown creatures, aggressive as he fights, and finally sad as he realizes he is mortally wounded.

Step 4

As a group, write a script, with each person contributing to their character's part. Add details to make each scene interesting and to build up the tension. Think about what the characters might say to one another, what they might notice, how they might comment on the mood, light, or setting, etc.

Step 5

Include a few stage directions in the playscript (remember, these can say what an actor does, or how he or she should deliver particular lines).

Step 6

Decide on how best to stage these events. Where are the entrances and exits? How can you show the audience the difference between the area outside the Manor and the space down in the cellar?

Step 7

Can you use different lighting to give atmosphere to the scenes?

Step 8

Are there any props that your characters need?

3　Present your mini-drama to other students and then ask them for feedback. What were the best bits? Which parts could be made more powerful?

● ●

Bram Stoker's novel, *Dracula*, was published in 1987. At that time, horror stories and tales of the supernatural were very popular and the novel was a great success. But the idea of vampires was not new. Legends about vampires had been rife for hundreds of years in Eastern Europe. In these legends, vampires appeared in various forms, including wolves and bats. They attacked their victims at night and feasted on their blood. The only way people could guard against vampires was to rub garlic round their homes and on themselves, or confront them with a cross.

1   Read this extract from Bram Stoker's novel, where Van Helsing is describing the vampire:

The vampire live on, and cannot die by mere passing of the time; he can flourish when that he can fatten on the blood of the living. Even more, we have seen amongst us that he can even grow younger; that his vital faculties grow strenuous, and seem as though they refresh themselves when his special pabulum is plenty. But he cannot flourish without this diet; he eat not as others. Even friend Jonathan, who lived with him for weeks, did never see him to eat, never! He throws no shadow; he make in the mirror no reflect, as again Jonathan observe. He has the strength of many in his hand ... He can transform himself to wolf ... he can be as bat ... He can come in mist which he create ... He come on moonlight rays as elemental dust ... He become so small – we ourselves saw Miss Lucy, ere she was at peace, slip through a hair-breadth space at the tomb door. He can, when once he find his way, come out from anything or into anything, no matter how close it be bound or even fused up with fire ... He can see in the dark – no small power this, in a world which is one half shut from the light. Ah, but hear me through. He can do all these things, yet he is not free. Nay, he is even more prisoner than the slave of the galley, than the madman in his cell. He cannot go where he lists; he who is not of nature has yet to obey some of nature's laws – why we know not. He may not enter anywhere at the first, unless there be someone of the household who bid him to come … His power ceases, as does that of all evil things, at the coming of the day.

2　This text was written over 100 years ago. Although the style of writing is different to modern writing, you can still understand what is being said.

Summarize this text by making a list, headed 'Features of the vampire'. It might begin like this:

Features of the vampire

The vampire does not die.

He thrives on the blood of living things.

He does not eat anything else.

He has no shadow.

He has no reflection in a mirror.

He is strong …

3   How does in this text differ from modern English? Think about:

   ● words and that we no longer, or rarely, use today
   ● words that we use differently today
   ● expressions that we no longer use
   ● whether the sentences are simple or complex/ short or long
   ● the use of semi-colons
   ● the verb endings (in particular, where we would put an 's' on the end of verbs to express the third person singular, e.g. 'The vampire live on …').

4   Using the information on your list, write a modern version of this passage. Is it longer or shorter than the original text?

5   Discuss the portrayal of vampires today (e.g. in the cartoon *Count Duckula*, and in the TV series *Buffy, the Vampire Slayer*). Think about books and films that have connections with vampires. Are these vampires frightening or comic? Do they share any of the same features as Bram Stoker's Count Dracula?

6 Do some research on the term 'gothic novel'. You might like to start by looking up the word 'gothic' in a good dictionary. This should give you at least the origin of the word. The Internet might give you further information. Find out:

- when gothic novels became popular
- titles and authors of other gothic novels (many are fairly long, but shorter adaptations are available)
- about other horror stories written by Bram Stoker.

FURTHER ACTIVITIES

1   The novel uses many diary extracts to tell the story. Imagine Dracula wrote a diary and write an entry for one night's activity. Use information from the playscript about how, when, where, and with whom the activity took place. Try to record Dracula's thoughts and feelings, as well as recounting his actions.

2   Choose a character in the play. Skim the playscript and gather information about your character. Think about their personality and their motives for their actions. Be prepared to role-play as your character, and answer questions, in character, during a hot-seat activity.

3   Write and design a programme for a stage production of *Dracula*. List the characters and scenes, and summarize the plot. Remember – you want to whet the audience's appetite for the play without giving away the whole plot!

4   Do some research on Bram Stoker, the author of the novel, *Dracula*. Find out about his career, his interest in the theatre, his other novels, and his links with Whitby.